# McGRAW-HILL READING

# Language Support

## Teacher's Manual

**Grade 4**  Lessons/Practice/Blackline Masters

**Macmillan McGraw-Hill**

New York    Farmington

# Table of Contents

## Grade 4

# Unit 3

# Unit 4

# INTRODUCTION

As a dynamic social process, learning calls for students and teachers to be partners. This Language Support Manual, which accompanies MCGRAW-HILL READING, was developed to help you achieve that partnership.

Throughout this Language Support Manual you will find strategies and activities designed to help ESL students become participants in classroom learning communities with their English-speaking peers. Based on current and proven methods for teaching ESL students, these strategies and activities reflect important ideas about the learner's role and about language and communication, which are at the heart of MCGRAW-HILL READING.

For ease of reference, this introduction is divided into two parts: the first part, **Teaching the ESL Student**, is designed to orient you to the unique needs of the ESL learner; and the second part, **Teaching the Reading Selection**, mirrors the corresponding lesson in the Teacher's Edition and offers suggestions on how to present the reading skills and concepts for classes with native speakers and second language students.

**Students and teachers are partners in learning.**

**Sheltered Instruction**

## Teaching the ESL Student

This section of the introduction will help you adapt your skills to meet the needs of the ESL student. Differences between teaching native English speakers and ESL students are linguistic, social, and cultural. It is not enough for ESL students to know the appropriate language to use in a given context, although this is certainly critical. In addition, you, as teacher, must ensure that ESL students are active and equal participants in the classroom. Students must be made to feel that their contributions are valuable even though they may only approximate native English speaker accuracy. They must also feel that their culture and prior experience have a respected place in the classroom.

In the following chart, we provide you with the characteristics of language learners in each of the four stages of second language acquisition. You will find it useful in identifying language behavior and building a profile of your ESL students. In the remainder of this section, we will outline procedures and activities for accommodating ESL students, strategies for meeting their unique needs, group interaction patterns that foster effective learning, the classroom environment, assessment tools, and social factors and their relevance to learning.

# Stages of Second-Language Acquisition

Like their English-speaking classmates, ESL students will be at different levels of language and literacy proficiency in their native language. They will also be in various stages of English language acquisition. This Language Support Manual lists teaching prompts at four different levels which follow the chart below and summarizes the four stages of second language acquisition. As your ESL students move through the four stages, this chart may be helpful in making informal assessments of their language ability and in determining which prompts you should use.

## Preproduction

**nonverbal prompt for active participation**

- Teachers ask students to communicate with gestures, actions, yes/no answers, and names.
- Lessons focus on listening comprehension.
- Lessons build receptive vocabulary.

(Reading and writing are incorporated.)

## Early Production

**one- or two- word response prompt**

- Teachers ask students to respond to *either/or* questions.
- Students respond with one or two word phrases.
- Lessons expand receptive vocabulary.
- Activities encourage students to produce vocabulary they already understand.

(Reading and writing are incorporated.)

## Speech Emergence

**prompt for short answers to higher-level thinking skills**

- Students respond in longer phrases or sentences.
- Teachers model correct language forms.
- Lessons continue to develop receptive vocabulary.

(Reading and writing are incorporated.)

## Intermediate Fluency

**prompt for detailed answers to higher-level thinking skills**

- Students engage in conversation and produce connected narrative.
- Teachers model correct language forms.
- Reading and writing are incorporated.

# Procedures and Activities

The teacher's role in the scaffolding process is to provide necessary and meaningful support toward each learning objective. The scaffolding process requires the student to take ownership for learning and the teacher to provide appropriate direction and support in teaching. It requires a form of collaboration between teachers and students in which both work together to ensure that students internalize rules and strategies for meaning-making. The following components of sheltered language instruction are methods which support the needs of second language learners and provide for optimal language arts learning.

- Reciprocal Teaching
- Cooperative Grouping
- Cross-age Tutoring

**Reciprocal Teaching**

Reciprocal teaching is one way to help ESL students successfully complete academic tasks. The process of reciprocal teaching involves structuring an interaction, assessing the student's comprehension from the response, and then restructuring the interaction to clarify or correct the student's response. As with other kinds of interactions in the classroom, *reciprocal teaching should be modeled and practiced as a whole class first, then it should be practiced in pairs.* The following are just some of the benefits which occur when this approach is implemented in the classroom.

- Teachers can show students not only what to learn but how to learn.
- Group interaction lends itself to varied learning styles.
- Students accept new responsibilities through a cooperative approach.
- Students' self-esteem is enhanced through shared responsibilities.
- Collaborative learning yields greater motivation, particularly for students at risk.

**Cooperative Grouping**

Through cooperative grouping, which is also very collaborative, students gradually assume responsibility for their learning. This approach is most effective when there is individual accountability. *Cooperative learning best provides the non-native speaker with opportunities similar to social experiences within which the native speakers have acquired the language.*

**Cross-age Tutoring**

The cross-age tutoring format provides yet another opportunity for students to study and learn together. *ESL students benefit from cross-age tutoring as they are engaged in focused conversation that will support their second language development.* Cross-age or peer tutoring has also been found to promote positive reading attitudes and habits.

Reciprocal teaching, cooperative grouping, and cross-age tutoring are approaches within the pedagogical framework of sheltered English instruction. The benefit of these varied grouping formats is that group members become interested in each other's opinions, feelings and interests. ESL students begin to feel more comfortable expressing themselves on the topic or in the presentation.

# Successful Group Interaction

*How do I insure that ESL students participate?*

**nonverbal prompt for active participation**

Being sensitive to the cultural backgrounds of ESL students is a critical function of the teacher. In many cultures, the teacher has absolute authority in the classroom and students play a relatively passive role. Students from such cultures may not participate as vigorously as their classmates.

**Elicit experiences that relate to students' native cultures.**

By creating a safe environment both in the classroom, and within the group structure, students will begin to participate more freely. You may facilitate this by eliciting experiences and including activities that relate to students' native cultures. For example, if you are discussing the weather, have students talk about the weather in their countries and ask them to bring in pictures that show the range of weather in their country. Ask such questions as: *Draw a picture of a rainy and cloudy day in your country.* This Language Support Manual offers many opportunities to incorporate individual cultural backgrounds. Every lesson includes activity suggestions and teaching prompts which introduce skills and strategies through a compare/contrast matrix in the **Evaluate Prior Knowledge** and **Develop Oral Language** sections.

*How should I group my native English students and ESL students for maximum learning and cooperation?*

**ESL students benefit from social interactions with native speakers.**

Social interaction plays an important role in language development. In group work, ESL students benefit from interactions with native speakers by having more chances to try out the language they are learning. But effective group work depends on careful organization, thoughtful selection of groups, and the active involvement of the teacher.

Additionally, the following chart details various strategies that can enhance both reading comprehension as well as the oral language proficiency of second language learners.

## Modeling

*How do I adapt my teaching methods to accommodate the ESL learner?*

**Illustrate the Concept**

In addition to traditional board work, ESL students need a significant amount more support and practice than native English speakers. Therefore it is essential that you give those students the necessary practice and it is vital that this support comes in the form of experiential and oral activities, before written work or reading. For example, writing the words *big* and *small* on the board and then asking students to name objects in either category, is not an adequate presentation for ESL learners. A more successful technique would be to illustrate the concepts through the use of physical objects in the room. For example, taking words that have already been associated with their objects, the teacher points to the larger of the two and says *This is big.* The students then repeat the phrase after the teacher's model. Next, the teacher points to the smaller object and says This is small. The students respond as

# A Pedagogical Overview of Strategic Sheltered Instruction

| SCAFFOLD | APPROPRIATE TASKS | | BENEFIT TO THE READER |
|---|---|---|---|
| **Modeling** | Teacher models task and provides examples. Individual/Group oral reading, repetitions. Direct experience through practice. | | Clarifies concepts<br>Provides understanding of objective |
| **Connecting Content** | Questions in:<br>  Think-Pair-Share<br>  Quick-Writes<br>  Brainstorming | Three-Step Interview<br>Anticipatory Charts | Addresses students' prior knowledge<br>Provides a personal connection between learner and theme of the class. |
| **Creating a Context** | Visualizations<br>Focus questions and:<br>  Use of manipulatives<br>  Self-involvement<br>Instructor provides an experiential environment.<br>Students demonstrate knowledge for authentic audiences. | | Enhances context and concept familiarity |
| **Bridging Concepts** | Compare/Contrast Matrix used as advanced organizer<br>Story Graph used to skim through a text | | Students gain heightened insight of the varied uses of the language.<br>Students develop connections between concepts. |
| **Perceptual Understanding** | Reciprocal Teaching<br>Self-monitoring<br>Self-assessment<br>Students discuss and model reading strategies | | Self-autonomy is fostered<br>Enhances students' knowledge of strategies through a conscious focus on the processes |
| **Extension** | Drama<br>Story Boards<br>Collaborative posters with text<br>Eye-witness accounts | Journal writing<br>Post cards/letters | Students extend their understandings and personal relevance as they apply information to novel formats. |

in the previous example. The teacher can then point to two other objects (or pictures), one big and one small. Given the teacher's cue, the students point to and classify the two objects as either big or small.

By assisting the learner in producing utterances beyond his or her capacity, you are providing 'scaffolding'—that is, the necessary support and guidance needed for the learner's growth. Through this collaboration of teacher and student, the student should progress towards greater autonomy and ownership of his or her language, thereby fostering greater self-esteem and independence.

## Total Physical Response

*What activities should I use to supplement teaching?*

ESL students need to cover concepts using a variety of sensory input. Total Physical Response (TPR) is a well-established and successful technique that links language to a physical response. The classic game of "Simon Says" is a vivid example. The teacher (or a student) can call out a series of

# Suggested TPR Commands

| | | |
|---|---|---|
| Stand up | Giggle | Turn your head to the *right* |
| Sit down | Make a face | Drum your fingers |
| Touch the *floor* | Flex your muscles | Wet your lips |
| Raise your *arm* | Wave to *me* | Blow a kiss |
| Put down your *arm* | Shrug your shoulders | Cough |
| Pat your *cheek* | Tickle your *side* | Sneeze |
| Wipe your *face* | Clap your hands | Shout *your name* ("help") |
| Scratch your *knee* | Point to the *ceiling* | Spell *your name* |
| Massage your *neck* | Cry | Laugh |
| Stretch | Yawn | Sing |
| Whisper *(a word)* | Hum | Hop on *one foot* |
| Step *forward* | Lean *backwards* | Make a fist |
| Shake your *hand* | (Name), walk to the door | (Name), turn on the *lights*. |

Source: Richard-Amato, P. (1996) Making it happen: *Interaction in the second-language classroom,* 2nd ed. White Plains, N.Y.: Addison-Wesley Publishing Group/Longman.

commands (i.e., "Simon says, touch your toes,") and students respond with the appropriate physical gesture—in this case, by touching their toes. The advantage of this technique is it links language to the "here and now," giving learners, especially at the early stages, a concrete forum for language practice.

Because of linguistic, social, and cultural differences, ESL students will probably not cover concepts as quickly as native English speaking students. The teacher must be patient with these students and give them extra activities with varied sensory input. As with all learners, varying the pace and type of sensory input is essential—both for accommodating the various learning style preferences and maintaining interest in the lesson.

# Connecting Content

*How do I know my ESL students understand me?*

**Don't assume that ESL students don't know the answer.**

When you question your students and get no answer don't automatically conclude that students don't know the answer. Adapt your questioning strategies to help ESL students understand what you say. Rephrase the question. Replace difficult vocabulary with words students know. Add context by using pictures, objects, graphic organizers to support meaning. Use gestures and facial expressions to cue feelings and moods. Draw analogies to past experiences.

# Creating A Context

The Language Support Manual includes several blackline masters which coincide with the skills and strategies being taught within a reading selection. The blackline masters provide manipulatives to help students explore and practice skills. Use of manipulatives helps to enhance context while building concept familiarity.

**Use of Manipulatives**

*How do I set up the classroom as a strategic learning environment?*

The environment of the classroom can have a great impact on students' ability to learn. The following are some ways to make the classroom environment more comfortable so that ESL students can get as much as possible out of their classroom experiences.

**The Classroom Environment**

Create areas in the room designed to give ESL students opportunities to use the target language. For instance, if you are teaching the names of fruits, set up a "fruit market" and have students ask the "shopkeeper" for the fruits they want to buy. They can talk about how the fruits look and taste, how to prepare them, and how much they cost.

**Special areas in the room provide chances for students to apply their English skills.**

Set up a learner library with favorite books the students have chosen. Provide a "discussion" area where ESL students may sit with native language speakers to discuss their favorite books or to read to each other. Seating arrangements should always provide for flexible grouping.

# Bridging Concepts

*How do I activate 'prior knowledge' for students from a different culture?*

**Allow ESL students to make connections for themselves.**

With native English speaking students, the teacher has common ground on which to activate the students' prior knowledge. Although American culture is very diverse, there are certain associations and symbols that are familiar to all those who live here. However, for the ESL student the teacher faces a difficult challenge—being able to activate the students' prior knowledge often without knowledge of the students' cultures. With ESL students, as with all students, the teacher should be sure to allow students to make connections for themselves. Often the teacher has a pre-determined idea of the connection and by imposing that notion on the student, he or she does not serve the students' needs to the fullest. It is important for ESL students to develop autonomy and self-esteem.

# Assessment

**Use alternative ways to assess ESL students' learning.**

*How do I assess ESL learners?*

When assessing ESL students' learning, you need to adapt your expectations of what constitutes an appropriate response. Assessment that relies heavily on a written test or questionnaire, on written answers or an essay, or on answering oral questions verbally, may present problems for ESL students. Some alternative strategies include the following:

**Invite students to draw, show, or point to objects.**

- Allow students to draw, show, or point to an object, a procedure, or an illustration, rather than write or talk about it.

**Your observations may serve as a form of assessment.**

- Use your own observations and interactions with the students as a basis for assessment.

**Students may perform activities to demonstrate their understanding.**

- Ask students to perform an activity that will show the application of a concept. For instance, say: *Show me how a tired person acts.*

# Teaching the Reading Selection to Students Needing Language Support

Each Language Support lesson in this Language Support Teacher's Guide mirrors the corresponding lesson in the Teacher's Edition of McGraw-Hill Reading. It either builds directly on that lesson, offering suggestions on how to adapt materials for students needing additional language support, or it offers alternative teaching and activities. The blackline masters following each lesson provide tools for students to use with alternative activities that develop skills and strategies taught in the lesson.

In this overview, the Language Support lesson described is from the grade one unit theme, Stories to Tell. The selection, *Sam's Song,* is the story of a young owl who learns to sing with her family. Variations on the lesson in Grades K, 3-6 are noted where appropriate.

# Focus on Reading

## Develop Phonological Awareness (Grades K-2)

**Help develop children's awareness of sounds.**

This part of the Language Support lesson is designed to help children develop their ability to hear the sounds in spoken language. These skills can be improved through systematic, explicit instruction involving auditory practice. Each selection in grades K-2 begins with a lesson designed to focus the children's attention on a particular phonological skill. In the grade one selection, for example, children are asked to listen for digraphs, *ch, wh,* and *nk.* As you read aloud the poem, "Lunch Munch," children are asked to clap their hands each time they hear a word that rhyme with *bunch.* The activity is repeated with the word *think.*

Children who may be having difficulty hearing these sounds are guided through an activity in which they make up a series of tongue twisters containing the digraphs. For example: *The child chomps on a chip.* Students listen for and identify the words in which they hear /ch/.

In these practical, learner-centered lessons from the Language Support Teacher's Guide, children are often asked to respond physically to the sounds they hear. For example, in this grade one lesson, they are asked to whistle, chomp, or blink when they hear words with *wh, ch,* or *nk.*

The Language Support Teacher's Manual identifies these activities as **TPR** (Total Physical Response).

**Total Physical Response**

One of the most successful approaches to teaching English to language support children is Total Physical Response. At the heart of this approach is the belief that children should be active participants—as both fellow learners and experts—in learning communities where language and content are developed together.

## TPR:

- is most appropriate for children just beginning to speak English. It recognizes that children will spend a period of time—the silent period—listening to English before they are able to speak it. Particularly focused TPR activities help ESL children learn vocabulary and concepts.

- recognizes that ESL children can understand physical prompts and can indicate their understanding through action before speech. TPR involves giving commands in which you model a physical action and to which learners respond with an action, one or two words, or short responses.

- allows children to involve their bodies and their brains in the TPR activity; they respond with the total body. The commands should be fun and should make the second language understandable.

As you work with children needing additional language support , you may find many other ways to use TPR prompts. As children continue to develop  their phonological awareness, they will be asked to identify rhyming words, listen for separate syllables in a word, separate the first sound in a word from the rest of the word, and blend sounds together to make words. Recent research findings have strongly concluded that  children with good phonological awareness skills are more likely to learn to read well. These lessons will help you work with children from diverse cultural and linguistic backgrounds as well as engage ESL children in productive activities to achieve literacy.

## Develop Visual Literacy (Grades 3-6)

The Language Support Manual expands this lesson by suggesting physical activities which help clarify the Comprehension Strategy Objective stated in the Teacher's Edition. This section also presents an opportunity to involve the ESL student with discussion prompts which explore the individual students cultural background and uses their prior knowledge to do a compare and contrast activity which will assist in introducing the lesson content.

# Read the Literature

*This section introduces the unit concepts and the vocabulary needed to understand them.*

## Vocabulary

Suggestions are given here for teaching the vocabulary strategies highlighted in the Teacher's Planning Guide. Notes may call attention to idioms, figurative language, or language special to the selection. The vocabulary words are included, together with questions and tips for helping children increase comprehension.

An example activity from the grade one lesson for *Sam's Song* follows:

> Invite children to play a game of "Find the Word." Organize the group into two teams. Write the vocabulary words on the board for both teams. Then invite one child from each team to the board and ask them to erase the word you call out. If a child erases the incorrect word, rewrite it. Play until one team erases all the words.

## Evaluate Prior Knowledge

Building background is particularly important when children's cultural diversity interferes with comprehension. It is equally important to bring the reading topic to life—give it some immediate relevance—when it is unfamiliar to those children.

**Recognize different prior knowledge bases; use familiar contexts to introduce unfamiliar topics.**

This section of the lesson includes activities to help children get to know something about the cultural traditions and beliefs that move the story along and that may influence characters' actions. It is important to remember that ESL children's prior knowledge bases were not developed around the cultural traditions of English. They need help developing strategies to activate their own prior knowledge, so crucial to constructing meaning. Recognize that it takes time to learn concepts using a familiar language, let alone a new one.

**Model the language and use props when possible.**

The activities in this section help ESL children deal with culturally unfamiliar topics by giving it a familiar context. The concept is brought to life as children are encouraged to draw upon their personal experience and knowledge to get the big picture. Role-playing, objects, story props, pictures, gestures, stories with practicable patterns, and story maps are used in many of the activities to help set the topic in a meaningful context.

The concept of learning something new is addressed in the grade one selection *Sam's Song.* An example from this section follows:

Ask children to name things they have recently learned to do or would like to learn to do. Write their responses on the chalkboard. Ask one child to work with you as you model teaching how to do one of the activities. For instance, you might help a child learn to tie her or his shoe.

Next invite children to work in pairs to learn something new from each other. They can learn something real, such as making a paper airplane, or pretend to learn something, such as how to drive a car.

## Develop Oral Language

In the grade one selection, *Sam's Song,* children build background by focusing on the concept learning something new. It is important to help children become active participants in learning and confident language users. The activities in this section offer opportunities for children to respond orally to activities more suited to their abilities.

This part of the lesson also offers suggestions for TPR commands you can use when teaching story concepts. Like their English-speaking classmates, ESL children will be at different levels of language and literacy proficiency in their native language. They will also be in various stages of English language acquisition.

## Guided Reading

**Preview, Predict, Read** In *Sam's Song,* children are guided through a picture walk of the book. As children are directed to look at the illustration, they are asked questions, such as: *What do Chuck, Mom, and Pop do under the moon? Who watches them sing? Why do you think Sam looks sad? What does Sam finally learn to do? How do you think he feels?* Based on the children's abilities, they are called on to give short answers.

**Graphic Organizer** A graphic organizer which follows each reading selection is designed to engage children in active learning. In the grade one selection, *Sam's Song,* a "Story Puppets" blackline master is available. Children are asked to color the pictures of Sam and his family and then cut them out. The pictures are glued to craft sticks and used as puppets. The children work in groups of four and use the puppets to act out the story as you reread *Sam's Song* aloud.

**Engage children in active learning.**

# Build Skills

**Blackline Masters**

This section contains directions for using the blackline masters as well as informal assessment suggestions.

## Phonics and Decoding (Grades 1-2)

This section of the Language Support lesson provides suggestions and activities to help children acquire phonics and decoding skills. Like other sections of the lesson, it follows the Teacher's Planning Guide materials, modifying them and adapting them where possible or providing alternative approaches to the skill that are more appropriate for second-language learners. It covers:

## Comprehension and Vocabulary Strategy

This section offers suggestions to help children develop comprehension and vocabulary skills throughout the selection. Lessons encourage you to ask simple questions that draw upon the children's own experiences, cultures, and ideas. The blackline masters give the students additional practice for each assessed skill introduced in the reading selection.

In the grade one selection, *Sam's Song*, the comprehension skill, Compare and Contract, is reviewed. Children are asked to use the story illustrations to help them find similarities and differences in the story. For example, children are directed to a page in the story, then asked: *Is Sam like the mouse? How is she different from the mouse?* Children then work in pairs to compare similarities and differences that they find.

## Informal Assessment

After each skill or strategy has been practiced with the blackline master the Language Support Manual includes an informal assessment activity which requires the students to return to the reading selection and apply the skill.

# THE LOST LAKE pp. 18A–41P

Written and Illustrated by Allen Say

## BUILD BACKGROUND FOR LANGUAGE SUPPORT

# I. FOCUS ON READING

## Focus on Skills

### Develop Visual Literacy

**OBJECTIVE:** Analyze character and setting

Have students look at the painting *Gathering Watercress on the River Mole.* Say to students: *Point to who is in the painting.* Write down their responses on the board and explain that these are the characters. Next say: *Point to the objects around the characters.* Help students make note of the grass, the river, and the trees. Explain that this is the setting. Then ask students to pretend they are the characters in the scene. Have volunteers position themselves in the class, as if they are in the painting. Invite them to talk about what they notice, think, and feel. Prompt their ideas with questioning such as: *What do you see? Are you cold or hot? What do you hear? How do you feel?*

**TPR**
Have students use gestures or hand signals to identify people or items they might see, hear, or feel in this setting.

# II. READ THE LITERATURE

### Vocabulary

**VOCABULARY**
compass
brand-new
muttered
darted
mug
talker

Write the vocabulary words on the board. Then display Teaching Chart 2 and read with students. Circle the vocabulary words and underline the context passages. Then act out each sentence for the students. Pretend to hold a *compass* and point north. You might act out putting on a *brand-new* pair of boots, walking in them, and having them hurt your feet. Quietly *mutter* the statement on the chart. Show the action of *darting* by moving quickly around the room. Take a sip out of an imaginary *mug*. Act out *talking* by taking on two different roles of people having a conversation. Ask students to guess what each word might mean. Write their suggestions on the board. Then invite volunteers to act out the words themselves. Encourage the class to "vote" on the right or wrong use of each word.

### Evaluate Prior Knowledge

**CONCEPT**

camping

Display pictures of camping equipment, such as sleeping bags, tents, knapsacks, cooking utensils, and hiking clothes. Talk about how and why each item is used. Give groups of students an opportunity to role-play a camping scene.

**TPR**
Use visual prompts to stimulate physical response.

### Develop Oral Language

Have students draw a camping picture. They might include maps, special equipment, animals, stars, and so on. Then have each student tell about her or his picture.

nonverbal prompt for active participation

one- or two-word response prompt

prompt for short answers to higher-level thinking skills

prompt for detailed answers to higher-level thinking skills

- Preproduction: *Show us* (point to class and self) *how you feel* (point to face) *about camping.*
- Early production: *Have you camped before? Where do you sleep when you camp? What do you do when you go camping?*
- Speech emergence: *What did you show in your camping picture? What is your favorite part about camping?*
- Intermediate fluency: *How do you feel about camping? What makes it fun? What might be hard about camping?*

## Guided Instruction

### Preview and Predict

Tell students that in this story a young boy named Luke comes to spend the summer with his father. Explain that at first, Luke does not have fun because his father is working all the time. Then say: *One day Luke's dad wakes up early to take Luke on a trip. Where do you think Luke and his dad might go?* Ask students to look for clues as to the kind of trip the father and son go on as you guide them through the illustrations in the story. Encourage verbal responses to the pictures by asking questions such as: *What are the boy and his dad doing at home? When do they go? What do they bring with them? What do they see? What looks hard about this trip? How do you think the boy and his dad feel at the end of the story?* Encourage students to make their own observations as you go along.

**GRAPHIC ORGANIZER**
Blackline Master 1

### Objectives

- To develop understanding of character and setting
- To reinforce events of the story
- To support discussion and verbal exchange

### Materials

One copy of Blackline Master 1 per student; pencils

Copy the setting and character chart on the chalkboard. Read the first three paragraphs of the story aloud. Point to Luke in the illustration on page 21 and ask, *Who is this?* (Luke). Then point to Luke's dad and ask, *Who is this?* (Luke's dad). Explain that these are characters. Write Luke and Dad in the chart under Characters. Then ask, *Where is Luke?* (at his dad's home) Explain that this is the setting and enter it in the chart under Setting. Then ask, *How does Luke feel at his dad's house?* (he feels bored) Write the answers in the chart on the chalkboard. As you continue through the story, have pairs of students work together to complete the chart on their blackline masters. Prompt them by asking questions as new characters and settings are mentioned. Encourage them to use a word or two to describe each change in character or setting.

Invite partners to interview each other about the story, asking questions specific to characters and setting, such as *Where are Luke and his dad now? How does Luke feel now? How does Luke's dad feel now?* Have reporters write each other's responses.

# III. BUILD SKILLS

## Comprehension

**CHARACTER AND SETTING**
Blackline Master 2

**Objectives**
• To analyze character and setting
• To develop creative thinking
• To support comprehension of plot events

**Materials**
One copy of Blackline Master 2 per student; pencils

Encourage students to review the story, and to think about how the two characters, Luke and his dad, react to what they find at the first lake. Have them write their findings on the left side of the chart. Discuss the story's characters, settings, plot events, and ending. Then invite students to think of a different event in the plot. On the right side of the chart, have them write how the characters might react to this different event, and how this event may have changed the story's ending. For prompts, ask questions such as: *How would changing what happens at the first lake change what the characters do? How might that change the ending?*

**INFORMAL ASSESSMENT**

To assess students' understanding of character and setting, turn to the illustration on page 22 and have them work in pairs to discuss what they know about the characters and setting from this picture. Take turns calling on pairs to hear their ideas. Then turn to the illustration on page 26 and ask pairs how the setting has changed and how the characters seem different.

## Comprehension

**MAKE INFERENCES**
Blackline Master 3

**Objectives**
• To make inferences about story characters
• To encourage critical thinking
• To understand simple sentences

**Materials**
One copy of Blackline Master 3 per student; scissors; paste or glue; pencils

Invite students to look over the two pictures and think about how Luke and his dad related to each other in each setting. Then explain that what a character says often tells something about how she or he is feeling. Help students read the sentences at the bottom of the page. Ask students to decide which statements reflect the feelings of each person in the pictures. Have students cut these sentences out and paste them in the space provided underneath the appropriate picture.

**INFORMAL ASSESSMENT**

Turn to page 30 and help students read the conversation between the two characters. Ask students how they think both the son and the father are feeling according to what they are saying. Repeat the exercise at the bottom half of page 34, beginning with, "You know something, Dad?"

# Vocabulary Strategy

## MULTIPLE-MEANING WORDS
Blackline Master 4

### Objectives
- To identify multiple-meaning words and determine their meaning
- To support hands-on learning
- To reinforce context clues

### Materials

One copy of Blackline Master 4 per student; scissors; paste or glue

Explain to students that some words have more than one meaning. Discuss each picture and read aloud the incomplete sentences below. Have students cut out the words at the top of the page and paste them in the appropriate spaces. If necessary, complete the first two sentences as a class. Encourage students to think of other meanings for some of these words For example, a *bit* is part of the bridle and reins for a horse. *I am beat* can mean *I am tired.*

### INFORMAL ASSESSMENT

To assess students' understanding of words with multiple meanings, turn to the text on page 36 and read aloud the first sentence of the second paragraph. Then write the following two sentences on the chalkboard and read them aloud: *The feather is light. Plants need light and water to grow.* Ask students which sentence uses the word light in the same way as the sentence in the story.

Name_____ Date_____

# Story Elements

| Setting | Character |
|---|---|
|  |  |

# Different Stories

Write a story that ends differently from The Lost Lake.

|  | **The Lost Lake** | **Your Story** |
|---|---|---|
| **Characters** | Luke and Luke's Dad | |
| **Setting** | The lake and the forest | |
| **Plot Events** | Luke and his Dad go hiking to look for Lost Lake. When they find it, it is crowded with people. They go on and find a quiet lake where there are no other people. | |
| **Ending** | Finding the quiet new "lost lake" together makes Luke and his Dad feel closer to each other. | |

# Alone and Together

**1.** Cut out the sentences below. **2.** Paste the sentences that express what the people in the pictures are saying to each other, below each picture. **3.** What do the words the characters say tell you about how they are feeling?

---

"I am bored."

"I cannot talk now, Son.
I have to work."

"I am having fun with you, Dad!"

"I am having fun, too, Son."

---

# What Do They Mean?

**1.** Cut out the words below. **2.** Look at the pictures and read the sentences under them. **3.** Paste the correct word to fill in each blank.

| bit | right | beat | left |
|-----|-------|------|------|
| bit | right | beat | left |

You _____ your pack behind!

No I did not, it is _____ here!

To go up the mountain, follow the trail on your _____ .

To go down the mountain, follow the trail on your _____ .

Hey! That bug just _____ me.

We should race! I bet I can _____ you to that stream.

We should rest in the shade for a _____ .

My heart sure does _____ hard when I run!

# AMELIA'S ROAD pp. 42A–65P

Written by Linda Jacobs Altman  Illustrated by Enrique O. Sanchez

## BUILD BACKGROUND FOR LANGUAGE SUPPORT

## I. FOCUS ON READING
### Focus on Skills

**OBJECTIVE:** Introduce problem and solution

**TPR**

### Develop Visual Literacy

Bring students' attention to the painting *Broadbottom, Near Glossop.* Point out the road at the bottom of the picture and model two fingers "walking" on the road. Ask: *What is a road for?* Explain that a road helps you get from one place to another. Invite them to try to track with their fingers the road's path from the bottom of the painting to the top. Ask students: *Is it easy to follow this road? Is it hard? What happens to the road?* Help students discover that the road twists and becomes hidden in some places, but then it shows up again nearby. Invite students to create a twisting road, using classroom materials such as desks and chairs. Explain that the problem is finding a way from one end of the classroom to the other. As students follow the classroom roads, create more "problems" by placing a desk in the way or changing the way the road turns. Ask questions such as: *How will you solve the problem of the desk being in the way?* (Example: Make the road go under it like a tunnel.)

## II. READ THE LITERATURE

### Vocabulary

**VOCABULARY**
labored
shortcut
occasions
rhythms
accidental
shutters

Bring in pictures or show illustrations from *Amelia's Road* that represent vocabulary words, such as migrant workers picking apples for labored, a birthday party for occasions, people beating drums for rhythms, and a person dropping something for accidental. On the chalkboard, draw a map showing a shortcut through the woods to a house with shutters. Write the vocabulary words on the board and model sentences which match the words with the pictures. Use the following sentences: *The workers labored all day picking the apples. Amelia took a shortcut to get home faster. Amelia's birthday was one of her favorite occasions. She tapped her foot to the steady rhythms of the drums. It was accidental that she/he dropped her/his _____. The house had shutters covering the windows.* After you say each sentence ask students to come to the board and match the vocabulary word to the appropriate picture.

### Evaluate Prior Knowledge

**CONCEPT**
migrant workers

Bring in photographs of migrant workers and their families both at work and at other moments in their lives, such as traveling, resting, eating, and playing. Identify these people as migrant workers. Ask students to describe what each photograph depicts. Help students understand that these people travel from place to place to find work. If possible, point to a map to show possible places a migrant worker might travel to. Talk about the kinds of jobs migrant workers do and why they are not able to stay in one place. Then ask: *Where do you think these people might live? Why? What might they do for fun? What might be hard about their lives? What might be interesting?*

**TPR**

### Develop Oral Language

Using the pictures as visual aids, invite students to work in small groups to act out a day in the life of a family of migrant workers. Help them mark the beginning, middle, and end of the story with morning, noon, and night.

| nonverbal prompt for active participation | • Preproduction: *Show us* (point to class and self) *how your day begins. Show us how you feel about what you do.* |
|---|---|
| one- or two-word response prompt | • Early production: *Do you work in just one place? Do you move around a lot?* |
| prompt for short answers to higher-level thinking skills | • Speech emergence: *What kind of work do you do? Where do you do this work?* |
| prompt for detailed answers to higher-level thinking skills | • Intermediate fluency: *How do you feel at the end of the day? How long have you been* (kind of work)*?* |

## Guided Instruction

### Preview and Predict

Tell students that in this story a young girl named Amelia is unhappy because she and her family are always moving from one place to another. Explain that she and her parents are migrant workers. They travel all over, finding what work they can before moving on to another place. Ask students: *How do you think it might feel to never stay in one place?* Then tell them that in this story, Amelia looks for a way to feel like she has a home. Say: *Amelia wants to find a place that feels like it could be her own. What do you think this place might be like?* Then take students on a picture walk through the story, stopping to prompt students to predict how Amelia will solve her problem of not feeling like she has a home. Ask questions such as: *Do you think Amelia enjoys working early in the morning? What kind of work does Amelia do? Do you think Amelia likes school? What does the landscape look like where Amelia is now? What is special about the place Amelia finds?* Allow students time to make their own observations as you go through the pictures.

**GRAPHIC ORGANIZER**
Blackline Master 5

### Objectives

• To develop understanding of problems and solutions
• To practice summarizing information

### Materials

One copy of Blackline Master 5 per student; pencils

Explain to students that most stories tell about a character or characters who face a problem and then must solve it. Sometimes, you must try different things in order to find a solution. With each attempt at solving a problem a different result, or outcome, occurs. As students read the story, have them stop to write on their charts the problem the main character is facing. Then encourage them to find and write what the main character does to solve the problem. Have students note the outcome of each attempt and the final solution. At the bottom of the page, tell students to write a sentence that explains how the character finally solves the problem. Invite them to share and compare their ideas with the rest of the class.

Have partners interview each other about a problem they have had, what they attempted to do, what the outcome was, and how they finally solved the problem.

# III. BUILD SKILLS

## Comprehension

**PROBLEM AND SOLUTION**
Blackline Master 6

### Objectives
• To reinforce understanding of problem and solution
• To develop understanding of plot
• To make inferences

### Materials
One copy of Blackline Master 6 per student; scissors, paste or glue

Explain to students that in Amelia's Road, the plot is the story of how Amelia solves her problem. Invite students to review Amelia's problem and locate the sad Amelia at the top of the blackline master. Then have them cut out the icons that represent the pieces to her solution. Next, have students paste the icons in the appropriate spaces along her accidental road. Encourage students to explain how these things helped Amelia find a solution to her problem.

**INFORMAL ASSESSMENT**

To assess students' understanding of problems and solutions, turn to page 46, help students read text aloud, and ask them: *What problem does Amelia have here?* After hearing students' answers, turn to the next page, read it aloud, and ask: *How does Amelia want to solve her problem?* Help students see that Amelia wants a home of her own some day.

## Comprehension

**REVIEW SUMMARIZING**
Blackline Master 7

### Objectives
• To make inferences
• To practice following directions
• To encourage critical thinking

### Materials
One copy of Blackline Master 7 per student; pencils

Explain to students that both the words and the pictures in this story provide clues about Amelia and her family. Have them look over the numbered sentences and their corresponding pictures on the worksheet. Then read aloud these two statements about Amelia and her family: *Amelia's family does not have much money. Amelia's family works hard.* Then ask: *Which numbered clues lead you to these two statements?* Have students decide which corresponding clues go with each statement. Be sure to let students know that some clues may go with both statements.

**INFORMAL ASSESSMENT**

Turn with students to pages 50–51 and read the text aloud. Ask students how they think Amelia feels about her life according to the text and pictures. Then have students turn to page 59 and read the first two paragraphs. Ask students to explain why Amelia puts these items in the box.

# Vocabulary Strategy

## Objectives

• To identify antonyms
• To develop word identification skills
• To increase vocabulary

## Materials

One copy of Blackline Master 8 per student; pencils; crayons

Explain to students that antonyms are words whose meanings are opposite each other. Read over the incomplete sentences with students. Have students choose the pair of antonyms listed on the top of the page that correctly fills in the blanks for each sentence. If necessary, model the exercise with the first sentence. Then invite students to draw pictures in the boxes to illustrate each sentence.

**INFORMAL ASSESSMENT**    To assess students' understanding of antonyms, turn to page 46 and read aloud the different kinds of roads listed. Ask students to match up the kinds of roads that are opposite each other. (straight and curved roads; dirt and paved roads)

Name_____ Date_____

# Problems and Solutions

### Problem

### Steps to Solution

### Solution

# Road to a Solution

1. Help Amelia find the solution to her problem. 2. Cut out the icons she uses as part of her solution. 3. Paste the art in the correct places along Amelia's road.

# Reading for Clues

**1.** What do these words and pictures tell us about Amelia and her family?
**2.** Match the numbers next to the sentences with the statements at the bottom of the page. **3.** Some numbers may go with both statements.

**1.** Amelia's father drives a rusty old car.

**2.** The family gets up at dawn.

**3.** Amelia grabs an apple for her lunch.

**4.** The family moves into an old labor camp cabin.

**5.** Amelia picks fruit before school.

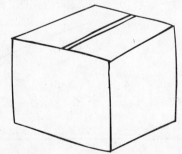

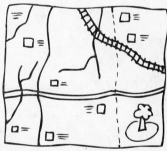

**6.** Amelia uses a box from the trash for her treasure box.

**7.** Amelia's family must keep moving from place to place.

Amelia's family does not have much money. _____

Amelia's family works hard. _____

# Picturing Antonyms

**1.** Choose the pair of antonyms below that goes with each sentence.
**2.** Write the words in the blanks. **3.** Draw a picture in the box that tells about the sentence.

| | |
|---|---|
| **bright/glum** | **trash/treasure** |
| **settle down/move around** | **straight/curved** |

**1.** One of these roads is _____.

The other road is _____.

**2.** He is feeling happy and _____.

She is feeling sad and _____.

**3.** One person's _____ is

another person's _____.

**4.** The dog wants to

_____ _____.

The cat wants to

_____ _____.

# SARAH, PLAIN AND TALL pp. 66A–93P

Written by Patricia MacLachlan  Illustrated by Burton Silverman

## BUILD BACKGROUND FOR LANGUAGE SUPPORT

## I. FOCUS ON READING

### Focus on Skills

**OBJECTIVE:** Analyze character, setting, and plot

**TPR**

### Develop Visual Literacy

Review with students the story elements of character, setting, and plot. Point to a student and say: *This is* [name of student]. Point to another student and say: *This is* [name of student]. Draw two simple pictures of the students on the chalkboard. Then ask: *Where are they?* Guide students to see that they are in the classroom, or in a school. Draw a school around the pictures of the students in the chalkboard. Explain that in a story, the characters are the *who* and the setting is the *where* and *when*. Explain that what happens to these characters is the plot of a story.

Show students the painting *Admiring the New House,* by Jane Wooster Scott, and read the title aloud. Then ask students to describe the setting. Ask: *What time of year does it seem to be? Does this scene take place in the present or long ago? How can you tell?* Next, point to various characters and ask: *Who do you think this person is? Do you think these people are related? What are they doing in the picture?* Finally, ask students what they think is happening. Point to the sign on the lawn and have a volunteer read what it says. When students have a full understanding of the painting's story elements, invite them to paint or draw pictures of another family and home, either their own or a place, and people from their imaginations. Let them tell about the setting, characters, and plot of their pictures.

## II. READ THE LITERATURE

### Vocabulary

**VOCABULARY**
overalls
eerie
huddled
squall
reins
pesky

To introduce vocabulary words, read the sentences from Teaching Chart 14. Ask a volunteer to pantomime the sentences as you read them. To reinforce understanding, show pictures, pantomime, or ask questions about each word. For example, show students a picture of overalls. For *eerie*, say: *She had an eerie feeling when she walked into the graveyard.* Then ask: *Is an eerie feeling a good feeling or a strange feeling?* For *huddled*, use student volunteers to show them huddled around a fire. For *squall*, show students pictures of violent storms. For reins, show a picture of a horse's reins. For *pesky*, say: *He was bitten several times by the pesky mosquito.* Then ask: *Is something that is pesky annoying or pleasant?* Then invite student pairs to make vocabulary cards, with a word on one card and a picture on another card. Guide them by providing example definitions and pictures on the chalkboard. Students can then mix up their cards and take turns matching each word with its picture or definition.

## Evaluate Prior Knowledge

**CONCEPT**

coming to a new home

Dramatize coming to a new home by entering the classroom with a suitcase full of clothes and a box full of household items. Make one corner of the classroom your new home and act out unpacking your belongings, hanging things up, and exploring the area. As you do these things, ask students to describe what you are doing. Continue the activity until students come to a consensus that you are moving into a new home. Ask students when people might move into a new home. Explain that families move because of jobs, individuals may move to go to college, or to be close to family. Invite students to pantomime moving into a new home. Students may wish to work individually, with partners, or in small groups to create situations similar to the one modeled by you. Have students consider what they would bring with them when they move, what they would unpack first, and how they would feel about what they left behind.

## Develop Oral Language

**TPR**

nonverbal prompt for active participation

one- or two-word response prompt

prompt for short answers to higher-level thinking skills

prompt for detailed answers to higher-level thinking skills

• Preproduction: *Show us* (point to class and self) *how you move into a new home. Show us the items you are moving.*

• Early production: *Have you ever moved before? Have you lived in your home for a long time? Would you bring your clothes to a new home? Would you bring your furniture?*

• Speech emergence: *What does your new home look like? What do you like most about it? Who moved with you?*

• Intermediate fluency: *How do you feel about moving into a new home? What was fun about moving? What was hard about moving? What is your new neighborhood like?*

# Guided Instruction

## Preview and Predict

Tell students that this story is about a woman from Maine who responds to an advertisement placed by a farmer to come take care of his children. Explain that the farmer's wife has passed away and that the farmer does not think he can raise his children by himself. Then turn to pp. 68–69 and read aloud the title. Point to the illustration and invite students to describe the woman. Ask: *Does this woman look like the woman described in the title?* Then lead students through the story illustrations, inviting them to make their own observations and predictions. Prompt students by asking questions such as: *What does life on a prairie farm seem like? Do you think this story takes place in the present, the past, or the future? Do you think Sarah fits in on the farm? Do you think it is easy or hard for Sarah to live in her new home? Who do you think are the other people in the picture? How do you think they look different from people today?*

**GRAPHIC ORGANIZER**

Blackline Master 9

## Objectives

• To analyze character and setting
• To distinguish between important and unimportant information
• To practice critical thinking

## Materials

One copy of Blackline Master 9 per student; pencils

Discuss the chart with students. Copy it on the chalkboard. Explain that they will use the chart to record details about the setting, what the characters want, the plot, and the outcome. Read the story as a group. At critical points, prompt students to discuss the setting and how it relates to what the characters want. Write the answers on the chalkboard and have students copy them on their blackline masters. At the end, have students discuss the plot problem and how it relates to the outcome.

# III. BUILD SKILLS

## Comprehension

### REVIEW STORY ELEMENTS
Blackline Master 10

**Objectives**
• To make inferences about and analyze character, setting, and plot
• To develop critical thinking
• To practice following directions

**Materials**

One copy of Blackline Master 10 per student; pencils

Invite students to recall the characters, setting, and events of the selection. Then help students read the words at the top of the page. Explain that some of these words refer to places or people in the past or far away and other words refer to people or places in the story now. Some words belong to both categories. First, have students find the people and places from the past or far away and list them in the left-hand circle. Then have students point to the people and places from the story's present and list them in the right-hand circle. Finally, challenge students to list items and people that belong in both circles.

**INFORMAL ASSESSMENT**

To assess students' understanding of character, setting, and plot, turn to the text on page 69 and read it aloud. Ask students: *Which character is from the past?* (Mama) *What place is far away?* (Maine) *Where is the story taking place?* (the prairie) *What is happening right now?* (Sarah writes in response to Papa's advertisement.)

## Comprehension

### REVIEW PROBLEM AND SOLUTION
Blackline Master 11

**Objectives**
• To review problem and solution
• To support comprehension of story concepts

**Materials**

One copy of Blackline Master 11 per student; oak tag; metal paper fastener; scissors; crayons

Review the worksheet with students and help them read any unfamiliar words. Then have students pair up with a partner. Tell students that some of the statements in the pie are solutions to Anna and Caleb's problem. The other statements would not help Anna and Caleb. Have partners color the solution pieces red and the problem pieces blue. Then ask students to cut out the circle and paste it to a piece of oak tag. Next, have them cut out the arrow and fasten it to the center of the circle with a paper fastener so it can spin easily. Finally, invite partners to play a game: Each partner takes six turns spinning. Whoever lands on solution pieces the most times, wins.

**INFORMAL ASSESSMENT**

Turn to page 71 and help students read through pages 73. Assess their understanding of problems and solutions by asking them why Sarah is sad (she misses Maine) and what Maggie does to help her. (brings her flowers to plant a garden) Repeat the exercise on page 79, where Sarah's chickens are left in the storm and she and Papa go out to rescue them.

**REVIEW SYNONYMS AND
ANTONYMS**
Blackline Master 12

### Objectives
• To review synonyms and antonyms
• To increase vocabulary

### Materials

One copy of Blackline Master 12 per student; pencils

Review with students that synonyms are words that have the same meanings and antonyms are words that have opposite meanings. Have them look over the two columns of words on their blackline masters. Ask student to draw solid lines between the synonyms and dotted lines between the antonyms.

**INFORMAL ASSESSMENT**

To assess students' understanding of synonyms and antonyms, turn to page 69. Point out the word ocean, and ask students to find a word on the same page that has the same meaning. (sea) Then turn to the next page and point out the word old in the paragraph beginning "Old Boss ...." Ask students to find that word's antonym in the same sentence (new).

# Analyze Character and Setting

## Setting

## What the Characters Want

## Plot Problem

## Outcome

# Past and Present, Near and Far

**1.** Think about the people, places and things that happened in the story, *Sarah, Plain and Tall*. **2.** Write the words where they belong in the Venn Diagram.

| | | | |
|---|---|---|---|
| the sea | Mama | a flower garden | Maggie and |
| the prairie | Sarah | horses | her children |
| the storm | chickens | Papa | the barn |
| | Seal the cat | | Sarah's brothers |

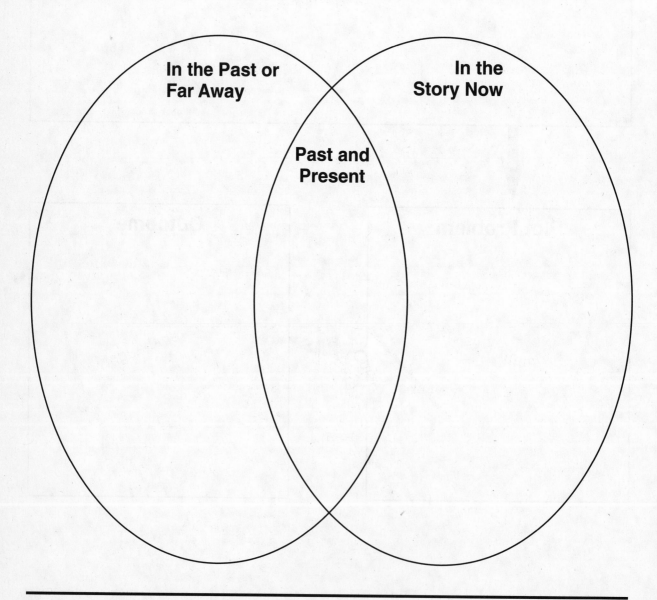

In the Past or Far Away

In the Story Now

Past and Present

# Spin for Solutions

1. Color the pieces that would help solve Anna and Caleb's problem *red*.
2. Color the pieces that would not help *blue*. 3. You and a partner take turns spinning the arrow six times each. 4. See who gets the most red pieces of the "pie" and solves the problem first.

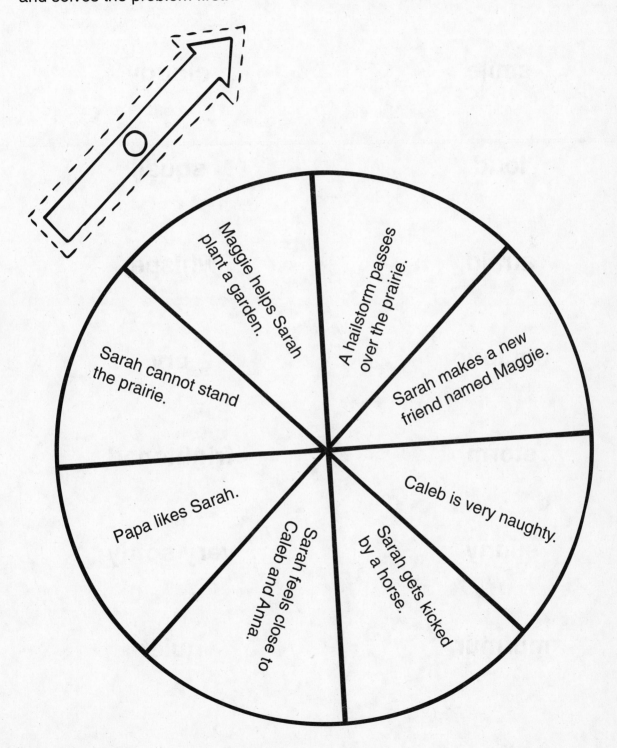

# Matching Game

**1.** Draw a solid line between synonyms (words that mean the same thing).
**2.** Draw a dotted line between antonyms (words that mean the opposite).

| | |
|---|---|
| smile | cloudy |
| loud | squall |
| afraid | whisper |
| out loud | cry |
| storm | frightened |
| sunny | very softly |
| murmur | quiet |

# SEAL JOURNEY pp. 94A–117P

Written by Richard and Jonah Sobol   Photographs by Richard Sobol

## BUILD BACKGROUND FOR LANGUAGE SUPPORT

# I. FOCUS ON READING

## Focus on Skills

### Develop Visual Literacy

**OBJECTIVE:** Identify main idea and supporting details

Bring students' attention to the quilt on pp. 94. Ask students to point out the items on the quilt as you say, people, animals, building, church. Encourage to see that more than one square may contain people or buildings or animals. Ask: *Do the squares have anything in common? Do the people and places look like people and places today?* Help students discover that together the squares tell of a time of the past, and that the quilt holds the details of this time and place together. Then invite

**TPR**

students to each create a square of their own and present it to the class. Explain that all the squares together make  a "quilt" to show what their lives are like. Decide together what main idea the collective quilt squares tell. Explain that each square is a different detail supporting the story of their lives.

# II. READ THE LITERATURE

### Vocabulary

**VOCABULARY**
jagged
horizon
squealed
nursery
mature
assured

Write the vocabulary words on the chalkboard. Use the words in the context sentences below, inviting children to guess their meanings. Write their suggestions on the chalkboard. Decide as a class which meanings are correct. Use the following sentences:

*The jagged ice looked like broken glass.*

*Looking across the horizon, we could see for miles.*

*The hungry baby seal squealed for its mother.*

*Thousands of seals are born on the ice every year. It is a giant nursery for baby seals.*

*The baby seals soon grow into mature seals.*

*The father assured his son that he would get to see the seals.*

Discuss nursery as a place where young living things are taken care of; use a tree nursery as a reference, showing pictures if possible. For example: *Here is a tree nursery. What is here?* Encourage answers such as baby trees or little plants. Then ask: *What is cared for in a seal nursery?*

For other vocabulary words, such as *squealed* or *mature*, provide synonyms such as screamed and grown-up. Encourage pairs of students to use all the vocabulary words in sentences of their own.

## Evaluate Prior Knowledge

Bring in photographs of harp seals, monarch butterflies, salmon, and Canadian geese. Have students form groups and choose one animal to research. Ask students to find out where the animals live, what they eat, and if they always stay in the same place. Have volunteers from each group describe what they learned about their animal. Then ask students if they know what these creatures all have in common. Help students understand that these animals all migrate, or travel from one place to another, during certain times of the year. Have students find a map and trace the animal's migratory journey on the map with their finger. Other students in the group can record information such as the time of year the animal migrates and how long the animal's journey is.

**TPR**
Have students use physical movements to track an animal's migratory pattern.

nonverbal prompt for active participation

one- or two-word response prompt

prompt for short answers to higher-level thinking skills

prompt for detailed answers to higher-level thinking skills

## Develop Oral Language

Have each group of students create their own migration maps for the animal they researched earlier. Encourage them to show as much information as they can, such as the distance traveled, time of year, time it takes to travel, and the purpose of the trip.

- Preproduction: *Show us* (point to self and class) *the kind of animal you learned about. Show us the path it takes as it migrates.*

- Early production: *Does (name of animal) travel a long way? Does it come back to its first home?*

- Speech emergence: *What does (name of animal) do when it reaches its new place? How long does it stay?*

- Intermediate fluency: *What would you like about being a (name of animal)? What would be hard?*

# Guided Instruction

## Preview and Predict

Read the title of the selection aloud and ask students: *What do you think this story will be about?* After listening to students' responses, confirm that this story tells about the journey that harp seals take to find a place to give birth. Explain that the author of the story is a photographer on assignment to photograph the birth and early life of harp seal pups. Pair English-speaking students with those needing additional language support. Begin a picture walk through the book, stopping to ask questions such as: *Describe the place where the seals are born. How do the author and his son get to the seals? What do the baby seals look like? What do the baby seals do?* Encourage students to share any previous knowledge they have of seals or migration with the rest of the class.

**GRAPHIC ORGANIZER**
Blackline Master 13

## Objectives

- To understand main idea and supporting details
- To summarize the main idea
- To encourage critical thinking

## Materials

One copy of Blackline Master 13 per student; pencils

Explain to students that the main idea of a story is the most important idea. The events or ideas that help explain the main idea are called the supporting details. Explain that some selections may have more than one main idea. Have students read the selection with a partner. As they read, lead them in a search to find and write the main idea and its supporting details on their charts. If necessary, copy the chart on the chalkboard and fill it in at appropriate times during the story.

Have partners work together to alternately find and write different main ideas and their supporting ideas within the story. Partners can share their findings with other pairs of researchers.

# III. BUILD SKILLS

## Comprehension

**MAIN IDEA AND SUPPORTING DETAILS**
Blackline Master 14

### Objectives
• To identify main idea and supporting details
• To understand sequence of events
• To support hands-on learning

### Materials
One copy of Blackline Master 14 per student; crayons; scissors; paste or glue

Ask students to review the main idea and details of Seal Journey, and to recall the order in which facts were learned. Then have students study the pictures on the blackline master and number them from 1 to 4 according to the order in which the events take place. Next, invite students to color the pictures, cut them out, and paste them together in the appropriate order to make their own seal book.

**INFORMAL ASSESSMENT**

To assess students' understanding of main idea and supporting details, turn to page 97 and read the text aloud. Ask students what the main idea is here. (The harp seal's life cycle is a wonder of nature.) Then ask what details support this idea. (These seals swim thousands of miles to give birth to baby seals.) Repeat the exercise on page 102 in regard to seals being great swimmers yet needing air to breathe.

## Comprehension

**MAKE INFERENCES**
Blackline Master 15

### Objectives
• To make and explain inferences
• To encourage critical thinking
• To follow directions

### Materials
One copy of Blackline Master 15 per student; pencils; crayons

Explain to students that the illustrations or pictures in a story often provide clues as to how a character may feel or what a situation might be. Have students look over the four pictures on the page and then think about what each character or creature may be thinking or feeling. Then have students create their own captions for each picture. Remind students that the captions should express what the picture shows about someone's thoughts, feelings, or actions.

**INFORMAL ASSESSMENT**

To assess making inferences, turn to page 99 and study the photographs. Have students use their own experiences as well as clues from the picture to determine how the person in the helicopter might be feeling. Repeat the exercise on page 105 with the bottom picture of the mother and baby seal.

# Vocabulary Strategy

## MULTIPLE-MEANING WORDS
Blackline Master 16

### Objectives
• To identify and understand homographs
• To reinforce vocabulary
• To read words in context

### Materials

One copy of Blackline Master 16 per student; pencils

Explain to students that homographs are words that are spelled the same but have different meanings. Invite students to think of the two meanings of each of the three words at the top of the page. Then tell students that each picture represents one of the two meanings of each word. Have students write the word that corresponds to each picture. Then ask students to use the same words to complete each sentence. When students are finished, encourage them to explain the meaning of each word in each context.

## INFORMAL ASSESSMENT

To assess students' understanding of homographs, turn to the text on page 103 and point out the word *ball*. Ask students to think of at least two different ways this word can be used. (e.g., to kick the ball; to go to a ball) Ask students what the word means here. Repeat the exercise on the same page with the word *back* (to lie on your back; to put something back).

# Main Idea and Supporting Details

| Main Ideas | Supporting Details |
|---|---|
| | |

# My Seal Book

**1.** Number the pictures in the order each happened in *Seal Journey*. **2.** Cut out the pictures. Color them if you want to. **3.** Paste the pictures together to make your very own Seal Book.

# If Pictures Could Talk

1. Each picture shows something that was described in *Seal Journey*.
2. Write a sentence under each picture that tells what each character in the story might be thinking. 3. Color the pictures.

# Alike But Different

**1.** The art below represents words that are homographs–they are spelled the same but they have more than one meaning. **2.** Look at the words. **3.** Write the word that corresponds to each picture. **4.** Then use the same words to complete the sentences below.

| rose | saw | seal |
|------|-----|------|

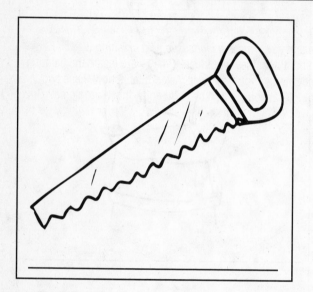

_____

_____

_____

**1.** I _____ my friend at the playground.

**2.** The girl gave her grandmother a _____.

**3.** We helped our brother _____ the envelopes.

# OPEN WIDE, DON'T BITE! pp. 118A–127P

## BUILD BACKGROUND FOR LANGUAGE SUPPORT

# I. FOCUS ON READING

## Focus on Skills

### Develop Visual Literacy

**OBJECTIVE:** Identify problem and solution

Show students the painting *Tiger,* by Kishi Ganku on page 118. Then ask students to use body language to tell what they know about a tiger, such as how it moves. Ask students: *What do you see here?* Help them see both the tiger and the crashing waves. For students needing language support point to the tiger and say: *This is a tiger.* Point to the landscape and say: *This is a landscape with crashing waves.* Encourage students to talk about how they would feel if they were inside the painting and were confronted by either the tiger or the waves. Ask students how these two

**TPR**

things might cause problems. What could a person do to solve those problems? Once ideas are generated, have groups of three act out a scene that includes the tiger or the waves, and a person facing one of the two forces. Encourage a second group to act out a scene that would be a solution to this problem.

# II. READ THE LITERATURE

### Vocabulary

**VOCABULARY**
fangs
reptiles
patients
skills
healthy
broad

Print the vocabulary words on the chalkboard. Then set up a corner of the classroom as if it were a dentist's office. Act out a scene in which you are a dentist explaining what your work is like. Use the vocabulary words in context to help students understand their meaning. For example: *Hello, I am a dentist. I had to learn many skills to become a dentist* (Pretend to work on a patient.). *Now I have many patients who need their teeth fixed* (Indicate a waiting room.). *Some of my patients are reptiles* (Show pictures or replicas of reptiles, and mime working on a reptile's mouth.). *I must be careful because a reptile's fangs are very sharp* (Point to the fangs in one of the pictures or replicas.). *Their teeth in the back, though, are broad and flat* (Spread your hands apart to indicate broad.). *I am very happy to be a dentist. I make sure my patients have healthy, strong teeth.* When you are done, ask students to take turns being dentists. Have them act out a new scene, using one of the vocabulary words from the board and saying it in a sentence related to the scene.

### Evaluate Prior Knowledge

**CONCEPT**
dental hygiene

Bring in various utensils related to dental hygiene, such as a toothbrush, toothpaste, dental floss, tooth picks, and nonalcoholic mouthwash. Also bring in a piece of fruit and a sweet that is not as healthy, such as a candy bar. Demonstrate taking care of your teeth by first choosing the healthier food, then brushing and flossing your teeth. As you act this out, ask students to describe what you are doing. Continue the exercise until students collectively conclude that you are doing things to maintain healthy dental hygiene.

## Develop Oral Language

Ask students to act out how they take care of their teeth at home. Make sure they are as specific as possible, and that they include kinds of food that are good and not good for their teeth.

nonverbal prompt for active participation

• Preproduction: *Show us* (point to class and self) *how you take care of your teeth.*

one- or two-word response prompt

• Early production: *Do you* (name dental hygiene activity) *after each meal? Have you been doing* (name dental hygiene activity) *for long?*

prompt for short answers to higher-level thinking skills

• Speech emergence: *When did you learn to take care of your teeth? What do you use to help keep your teeth clean?*

prompt for detailed answers to higher-level thinking skills

• Intermediate fluency: *Why do you think it's important to keep your teeth clean and healthy? What might happen if you don't?*

## Guided Instruction

### Preview and Predict

Explain to students that this selection is about a dentist who takes care of all kinds of animals. Have a volunteer read aloud the title and ask for students to explain its significance. After listening to their answers, have students look at the photographs and name the animals shown. Then ask: *What other kinds of animals do you think the dentist takes care of?* Write students' answers on the chalkboard, and return to them once the story is read so students can compare their predictions to the real answers. Also ask students to talk about the kinds of tooth problems various animals might have. On the second spread of the selection, have students predict what the purpose is of the tools shown and why the gorilla's hand is being held by a human hand.

**GRAPHIC ORGANIZER**
Blackline Master 17

### Objectives

• To reinforce understanding of problems and solutions
• To practice critical thinking

### Materials

One copy of Blackline Master 17 per student; pencils

Have students use the Problem and Solution chart to note the problems animals may have with their teeth and the solutions the dentist can supply. Have students use the chart to write problems the animal dentist may have with her or his patients.

# III. BUILD SKILLS

## Comprehension

**REVIEW MAIN IDEA AND SUPPORTING DETAILS**
Blackline Master 18

### Objectives
• To reinforce main idea and supporting details
• To encourage critical thinking
• To practice following directions

### Materials
One copy of Blackline Master 18 per student; scissors; paste or glue

Help students see that the blocks the dentist is standing on represent the main idea and the supporting details of the story. Ask them which block states the main idea (the top one). Lead students to understand that the remaining blocks represent details from the story that support the main idea. Then invite them to cut out the pictures from the bottom of the page. Have students paste only those pictures that represent animals mentioned in the story in the appropriate blocks.

**INFORMAL ASSESSMENT**

To assess students' understanding of main ideas and supporting details, turn to page 121 and help students read aloud the second and third paragraphs. Ask students to identify the main idea (Dr. Kertesz is a dentist who treats animals.) and any supporting details (He has worked on different kinds of cats.). Then turn to page 122 and ask how the photographs shown support the main idea. (They show what is involved in treating animals.)

## Vocabulary Strategy

**REVIEW MULTIPLE-MEANING WORDS**
Blackline Master 19

### Objectives
• To recognize words with multiple meanings
• To increase vocabulary
• To develop critical thinking

### Materials
One copy of Blackline Master 19 per student; pencils

Review with students the fact that some words have the exact same spelling but different meanings. Have students read over the unfinished story and then choose from the top of the page the multiple-meaning word or words to complete each sentence.

**INFORMAL ASSESSMENT**

Turn to the inset on page 122 and bring students' attention to the word *sink* in the subtitle. Ask students if they can think of two different meanings for this word. Then have a volunteer read the sentence aloud. Ask students which meaning the word has in this situation. Next, turn to the following page and have students identify other multiple-meaning words in the paragraph beginning, "One bad tooth can keep a tiger from hunting ...," such as *can* and *mean*.

**REVIEW SYNONYMS AND ANTONYMS**
Blackline Master 20

## Objectives

- To develop understanding of antonyms
- To use illustrations
- To support hands-on learning

## Materials

One copy of Blackline Master 20 per student; pencils

Ask students to look over the pictures and the list of words. Explain that each picture shows two images that are opposites and that within the list, each word is an antonym to another word also appearing there. Have students choose and copy in the appropriate spaces the pair of antonyms that fits the pictures.

**INFORMAL ASSESSMENT**

Turn to page 122 and help students read aloud the bulleted paragraph, beginning, "Cats and dogs have both kinds of teeth ...." Ask students to identify two words with opposite meanings (sharp, flat). Then help students read the top paragraph on page 123. Point out the word easiest and ask a volunteer to define the word. Then ask what word in the same paragraph has the opposite meaning (toughest).

# Problem and Solution

| Problem | Solution |
|---|---|
| | |

# Circus Act

**1.** Look at the animals at the bottom of the page. **2.** Which of these animals did you NOT read about in *Open Wide, Don't Bite!*? **3.** Cut out the animals from the story. **4.** Paste them on the page.

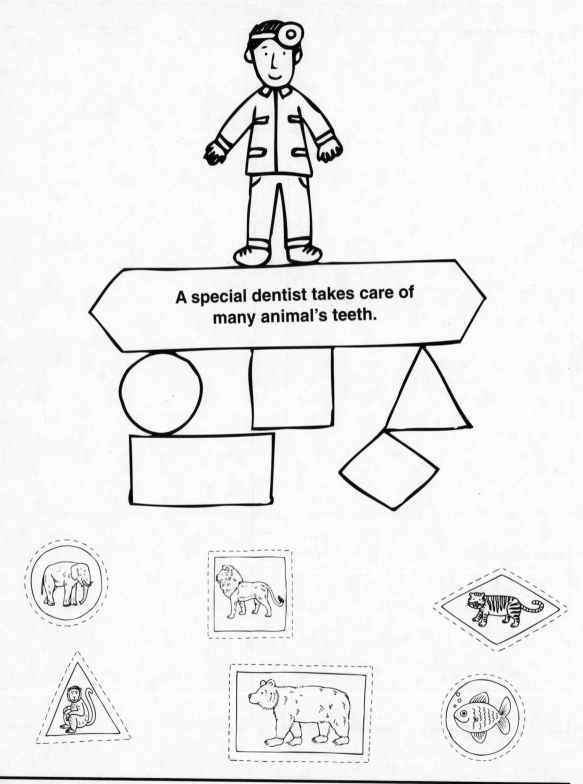

A special dentist takes care of many animal's teeth.

# A Silly Animal Story

**1.** Read the story below. **2.** The words listed in the box below each have more than one meaning. **3.** Use them to fill in the blanks and complete the story.

| pull | room | room |
|------|------|------|
| mean | pull | pull |
| bear | bear | mean |

The dentist opened her door and – surprise – into the _____

came a little boy leading a big, hairy _____.

"Goodness!" cried the dentist, "What do you _____ by bringing

that animal in here? Are you trying to _____ some kind of

joke on me?"

"No," said the boy, "He has a toothache. I think you will have to

_____ out his tooth."

"Well, all right," said the dentist. "Stand back and give me plenty of

_____." She held the creature down.

"Oh," cried the boy, "I can not _____ to watch!"

"I am not trying to be _____," said the dentist, "but this will

hurt." When he heard that, the creature roared, jumped up and ran out.

"Humph!" said the dentist, "That is not a _____ you have

there. If you ask me, it is just a big chicken!"

# Animal Opposites

**1.** Look at the pictures below. Each one shows two opposites. **2.** Find the pairs of words in the list that describe the two opposites in each picture. **3.** Copy the two words onto the lines under the pictures.

| | | | |
|---|---|---|---|
| **small** | **strong** | **sick** | **big** |
| **healthy** | **flat** | **weak** | **pointed** |

_____

_____

_____

_____

_____

_____

# JUSTIN AND THE BEST BISCUITS IN THE WORLD pp. 132A–157P

Written by Mildred Pitts Walter   Illustrated by Floyd Cooper

## BUILD BACKGROUND FOR LANGUAGE SUPPORT

## I. FOCUS ON READING

### Focus on Skills

### Develop Visual Literacy

**OBJECTIVE:** Make predictions

Bring students' attention to the artwork *Pictorial Navajo Rug*, by Betty Patterson. Encourage students to point to objects in the picture as you ask: *How do the people travel? What is the man in the far right-hand corner doing? What kind of animals do you see in the picture?* Tell students: *We might never know what will happen, but we can guess based on what we see and know.* Point to the person weaving the rug and say: *We can predict that the person will finish weaving the rug.* Then point to other objects in the picture and ask students to describe or pantomime what will happen. Point to a sheep and say: *What will happen to the wool on the sheep? What will happen to the baby? What will the cows be used for? How will the car change the way the people travel?* Finally, invite students to draw their own pictures showing a certain lifestyle and one thing within the picture that may cause a change. Have partners examine each other's pictures and predict what may happen.

**TPR**
Have students point to and discuss pictures to aid in understanding.

## II. READ THE LITERATURE

### Vocabulary

**VOCABULARY**
festival
resounded
pranced
inspecting
lingered
guilt

Write the vocabulary words on the board and point to each one as you read the sentences on Teacher Chart 32. Introduce the vocabulary words for this story by reading the sentences on Teacher Chart 32. Emphasize the vocabulary word and repeat the underlined context clues. Ask volunteers to act out the context clues and invite students to suggest definitions. Write their suggestions on the board and ask volunteers to replace the vocabulary word in the sentence. Have students decide which definition is the best. Then have them pair up and form questions with the vocabulary words. For example, *What do you do at a festival?* Then encourage students to meet with other pairs and take turns answering each other's questions.

### Evaluate Prior Knowledge

**CONCEPT**
cowboys

Bring in a photograph of a cowboy and a photograph of a business person in the city. Engage students in a discussion about how the cowboy is different from the city person, including clothing, work, transportation, living space, and lifestyle. Write students' ideas in a two-column chart on the chalkboard. Label the left column *Cowboy* and the right column *City Person*.

### Develop Oral Language

Have students create dioramas showing a scene of a day in the life of a cowboy. If students wish, they can work in pairs or groups of three. Allow students time to visit and compare each other's dioramas.

• Preproduction: *Show us* (point to class and self) *one thing cowboys do.*

• Early production: *Have you ever met a cowboy? Have you ever been to a ranch?*

• Speech emergence: *What do cowboys do? Where do they do their work?*

• Intermediate fluency: *How do you think cowboys feel about the work they do? Where do you think they learn to do their work? Would you like to be a cowboy or cowgirl? Why or why not?*

## Guided Instruction

### Preview and Predict

Turn to the first two pages of the story and have a volunteer read aloud the title. Tell students to look at the picture and ask: *How do you think the two characters in the picture know each other? Why are they on horses? Who do you think lives in the house in the background? Who do you think Justin is?* Then read aloud the introduction on p. 134. As you move through the story, allow students time to look at the illustrations and make their own observations about the characters, their actions, and the setting. Remind students of the story's title, and encourage them to look for illustrations that may provide clues as to its significance. After they have looked through all the illustrations, ask students if they think this story is just about biscuits. Ask them what else they think the story is about.

### Objectives

• To develop understanding of predictions
• To encourage critical thinking
• To organize information

### Materials

One copy of Blackline Master 21 per student; pencils

After reading the introduction, ask students to look at the first page of the story and predict what will happen. Ask: *What do you think Justin will learn from his grandfather?* Have students write their ideas in the left column of the chart. As they read, have them stop to fill in the chart with what really happens. Encourage students to stop at various points in the story to make other predictions and then fill in the *What Happened* column. If necessary, pair children needing language support with more fluent readers and writers.

# III. BUILD SKILLS

## Comprehension

**REVIEW MAKE PREDICTIONS**
Blackline Master 22

### Objectives

• To make predictions about a story
• To reinforce critical thinking
• To work collaboratively with others

### Materials

One copy of Blackline Master 22 per student; pencils

Explain to students that when reading a story, they can predict what will happen next by thinking about the information they have already read and by thinking about their own experiences. They can also use this information to predict what will happen after the story is over. Organize students into pairs. Have one partner read aloud the four possible outcomes of the story as written in the crystal ball. Have the other partner predict which outcome seems the most likely. Then have partners work together to list four events within the story that support the prediction they selected. Invite partners to share their findings with the rest of the class.

**INFORMAL ASSESSMENT**

Direct children to the illustration on page 217. To assess students' knowledge of predicting, have them pretend that Justin's shirts were still wrinkled just before the festival. Ask, *What do you think Justin would do?* If necessary, prompt, *What other chore might Justin's grandfather teach Justin?* (ironing)

## Comprehension

**INTRODUCE FORM GENERALIZATIONS**
Blackline Master 23

### Objectives

• To identify and form generalizations
• To practice critical thinking
• To support hands-on learning

### Materials

One copy of Blackline Master 23 per student; scissors; paste or glue

Explain to students that certain events and ideas can be put together to form generalizations, or general ideas about people, places, or things. Have students read the sentence printed in bold at the top of the page. Then ask students to read the sentences in the biscuits. Ask students to decide which statements go together to form the idea of the statement printed in bold. Have students cut only those statements and paste them on the plate in the outlines provided.

**INFORMAL ASSESSMENT**

To assess students' understanding of generalizations, turn to the top of page 144 and help students read aloud the paragraph beginning with *First they collected twigs and cow dung.* Ask students: *What generalization does Grandpa make here?* (Cow chips are the best fuel.) Ask students what ideas or experiences Grandpa probably had in order to make that generalization. (Grandpa has probably tried different materials to use as fuel and found that cow dung works the best.)

# Vocabulary Strategy

## INTRODUCE CONTEXT CLUES
Blackline Master 24

### Objectives
• To use context clues to find the meaning of specialized vocabulary
• To identify unfamiliar words
• To follow directions

### Materials

One copy of Blackline Master 24 per student; scissors; paste or glue

Tell students that the meaning of an unfamiliar word can often be understood by looking at its context, or the words surrounding it. Tell students that pictures can also give clues to word meanings. Have students read the sentences and study the pictures. Point out that the words on the worksheet all relate to work that many cowboys do. If necessary, read the sentences aloud with children. Explain that the underlined words appear in the story and that the circled words are clues to help understand the underlined words' meanings. Invite students to cut out the underlined words and paste them onto the pictures next to the things they describe or refer to.

## INFORMAL ASSESSMENT

Turn to page 138 and help students read aloud from the top to the paragraph beginning *Justin tried it.* Point to the word *rumpled* and ask students its meaning. Encourage students to identify clues from both the text and the accompanying illustration to conclude that *rumpled* means "wrinkled."

# Make Predictions

| Predictions | What Happened |
|---|---|
|  |  |
|  |  |

# Can You Predict the Future?

**1.** Read the sentences in the crystal ball to see what might happen to Justin.
**2.** Write what you think might happen. **3.** Share your idea with a partner.

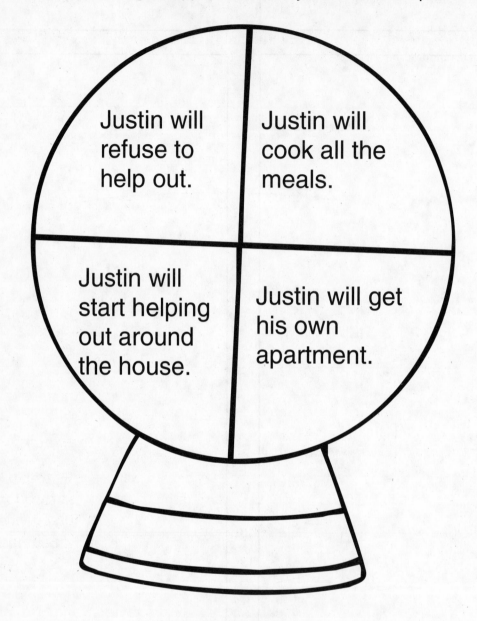

Justin will refuse to help out.

Justin will cook all the meals.

Justin will start helping out around the house.

Justin will get his own apartment.

**Story Events:**

1. _____

2. _____

3. _____

4. _____

# Fill up the Plate

**1.** Read this sentence:

*Men and boys are good at housework and cooking.*

**2.** Which four biscuits below the plate go together to make this sentence true?

**3.** Cut out the biscuits and paste them on the plate.

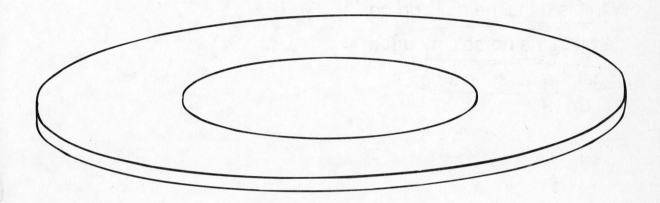

| | | |
|---|---|---|
| Grandpa made delicious biscuits. | Jessie Stahl was a famous Black cowboy. | Grandpa showed Justin how to make a bed neatly. |
| Justin saw how well Grandpa washed the dishes. | Grandpa and Justin were going to a rodeo. | Justin quickly learned how to fold up his clothes. |

# Get the Picture

**1.** Read each sentence below. **2.** Study the underlined words. These words appear in the story, *Justin and the Best Biscuits in the World.* **3.** Look at the circled words. These words are clues to help you learn what the underlined words mean. **4.** Cut out the underlined story words. **5.** Paste them next to the thing in the picture each word tells about.

The cowboy's <u>saddlebags</u> are on his horse, full of supplies. With his reins, he pulls up on the <u>bit</u> in the horse's mouth to signal the horse to stop.

The <u>broncobuster</u> is riding a kicking Brahma bull.

# JUST A DREAM pp. 158A–189P

Written and Illustrated by Chris Van Allsburg

## BUILD BACKGROUND FOR LANGUAGE SUPPORT

## I. FOCUS ON READING

### Focus on Skills

**OBJECTIVE:** Identify sequence of events

**TPR**
Tape the cards to students' shirts, and invite them to arrange themselves in order.

### Develop Visual Literacy

Turn students' attention to the photograph from the movie *The Wizard of Oz*. Explain to them that this scene shows just one moment in a long story. Ask students if they know what happened before this scene and what happened after. Ask, *Where do you think the characters are going? How do you think they will get there?* Write correct answers on the chalkboard. Then invite students to create two drawings based on what they know or what they imagine may have happened before this scene from the *Wizard of Oz*. Use questions to prompt students such as: *What happened before they got here? What happens when they get to Oz?* Have students trade their drawings and challenge each other to arrange them in the correct sequence.

## II. READ THE LITERATURE

### Vocabulary

**VOCABULARY**
foul
bulging
crumpled
haze
waddled
shrieking

Print each word on a flashcard. Display the flashcard for a word as you say it aloud and read the corresponding sentences from Teacher Chart 38. Have students turn back to the Visual Literacy photo and ask the following: *Do you think the flowers in the photo smell good or foul? What kind of face do you make when you smell something foul? What is the scarecrow made of? Are his clothes bulging with hay? What would happen if you took too much hay out of the scarecrow? Would he look crumpled like a piece of paper? Dorothy and her friends see the Emerald City through the clouds and haze. What would happen if there was too much haze? Would the Emerald City be easier or harder to see? What do you think Dorothy's dog, Toto, would do if a duck waddled by? Can you show me how the duck waddled? If the witch showed up, do you think the lion would run shrieking into the woods? What does shrieking sound like?*

Line the flashcards up on the chalkboard ledge in random order. Repeat the sentences, this time leaving out the vocabulary word. Ask pairs of students to come forward to select the correct flashcard. Encourage the students to act out the words when necessary.

### Evaluate Prior Knowledge

**CONCEPT**
ecology

Provide photographs of the following environments: mountains, lakes, rivers, oceans, trees, and so on. Explain that all of the things pictured make up our environment, or the place where we all live. Then tell students that ecology is the relationship between living things, such as humans and animals, and their environment. Demonstrate the concept of being ecologically responsible. Point to any signs or rules posted in the classroom for the removal of garbage or recyclables. Pantomime actions: put recyclable goods into various appropriate recycling bins; put trash in a garbage can rather than on the floor; turn off the light as you leave the room; act out riding a bicycle rather than driving a car. Ask students what you are doing. Repeat the activities until students understand that you are trying to take care of the environment. Talk about why it is important that all people work together to take care of the environment.

## Develop Oral Language

Invite students to pantomime ways that they can be ecologically responsible at home. Students may wish to work in small groups or individually to create situations such as those modeled by you.

- Preproduction: *Show us* (point to class and self) *one way to help keep Earth clean.*

- Early production: *Do you* (name activity) *every day? Is it something you do alone or with a friend?*

- Speech emergence: *What do you do to help keep Earth clean? Who taught you to do it?*

- Intermediate fluency: *How do you feel about (activity)? Why is it important? What else can you do to help keep Earth clean?*

# Guided Instruction

## Preview and Predict

Turn to the title page of the story and ask students to look carefully at the illustration. What do they see? Help them notice the piece of litter on the ground and the young boy walking away from it. Ask: *Who do you think left that garbage there? What do you think will happen to it?* Listen to students' answers, and then explain that in this story, the young boy in the picture dreams about a future world ruined by pollution. Ask students what might happen to the world if no one cared about the environment. Write their answers, and then guide students on a picture walk through the book. Give them time to observe the illustrations and to confirm or add to their predictions. Call their attention to the smaller illustrations that hint at what is coming next. You may also wish to ask at each new scene: *What caused this to happen?* Also, invite students to express how they think the boy may feel about what he sees. Finally, ask students what they think will happen when the boy wakes up.

**GRAPHIC ORGANIZER**
Blackline Master 25

## Objectives

- To identify the sequence of events in a story
- To encourage critical thinking
- To practice summarizing events

## Materials

One copy of Blackline Master 25 per student; pencils

Remind students that the sequence of events in a story is the order in which things happen. Have students write two events that happen at the beginning of *Just a Dream* on the chart. As students read, have them complete the chart with events that happen in the middle and near the end of the story. To further reinforce sequencing, invite students to write the sequence of events for one particular scene, such as Walter up in the tree or at his birthday party.

# III. BUILD SKILLS

## Comprehension

### REVIEW SEQUENCE OF EVENTS
Blackline Master 26

**Objectives**
- To identify sequence of events
- To work collaboratively with others
- To organize information

**Materials**

One copy of Blackline Master 26 per student; scissors; paste or glue

Have students work in pairs to review the events of *Just a Dream* and the order in which they occurred. Then invite partners to work together to cut out the phrases on the worksheet and paste them on the ladder in the proper sequence. Tell them to place the first event on the bottom rung of the ladder and the last event on the top rung. When they are finished, have different pairs look at each other's work and review the story to check for proper sequence.

**INFORMAL ASSESSMENT**

To assess students' understanding of sequence of events, turn to the illustration on page 169 and ask students to recall what is happening now, what happened just before, and what will happen next. Repeat the exercise on page 171.

## Comprehension

### REVIEW FORM GENERALIZATIONS
Blackline Master 27

**Objectives**
- To form and support generalizations
- To increase vocabulary
- To develop critical thinking

**Materials**

One copy of Blackline Master 27 per student; pencils

Explain to students that a generalization is a broad statement that can be supported with specific examples. Tell students that each sentence on their blackline master is an incomplete generalization. Read aloud the sentences with students. Then go over the words at the top of the page. Have students use what they have read and what they know to complete each generalization with a word from the top of the page.

**INFORMAL ASSESSMENT**

Turn to the illustrations on pages 164, 166, 168, 170, 172, 174, 176, and 178. On each page, ask students what is happening in Walter's dream. After looking at the last picture, ask students: *What generalization can we make from these different scenes about Walter's dream?* (It was a bad dream about pollution.)

# Vocabulary Strategy

## INTRODUCE COMPOUND WORDS
Blackline Master 28

### Objectives
• To identify and determine the meanings of compound words
• To increase vocabulary
• To follow directions

### Materials

One copy of Blackline Master 28 per student; pencils

Explain to students that compound words are words formed by joining two smaller words. Tell students that the story *Just a Dream* contains many compound words. Invite students to look at the pictures in the two columns and try to find the corresponding words in the list below. You may want to discuss the pictures with students and read aloud the listed words. Then have students draw lines to connect the two pictures that go together and write the compound word that goes with them on the corresponding line. If necessary, tell students that the picture representing the first part of each word is always in the left column.

## INFORMAL ASSESSMENT

To assess students' understanding of compound words, turn to page 168 and point out the word *workman*. Ask students to decipher its meaning by finding the two words that create it. (work and man) Repeat the exercise on page 180 with the word *snowflake*.

# Sequence of Events

# Up a Tree

**1.** Cut out the places where Walter goes in his dreams. **2.** Paste them on the ladder in the order they happened in the story. **3.** Stop when you get to the top of the tree.

In his dream, Walter finds himself:

| at the dump | at the Grand Canyon | on the ocean | at a factory |
|---|---|---|---|
| in the sky with ducks | on Mt. Everest | on a highway | in a tree |

# What Would Happen?

Fill in the blank in each sentence with a word or words from the list below.

| forest | polluted | garbage dump | stopped |
|---|---|---|---|

**1.** If everyone threw trash on the ground, the earth would soon be a huge

_____.

**2.** If everyone cut down a tree, the earth would soon not have one

_____.

**3.** If everyone drove cars, traffic on the highways would soon be

_____.

**4.** If every car and factory made bad smoke, the air would soon be

_____.

# All Together Now

1. Look at the pictures. 2. Find the word below that goes with each picture.
3. Write a line connecting two pictures that go together to make one compound word. (Hint: All the pictures in the left column show the first part of a word.)
4. Write the compound word on the line next to the pictures.

| wood | birth | pick | cutter |
|------|-------|------|--------|
| smoke | boy | day | cow |
| post | card | tack | tooth |

_____

_____

_____

_____

_____

# LEAH'S PONY pp. 190A–215P

Written by Elizabeth Friedrich  Illustrated by Michael Garland

## BUILD BACKGROUND FOR LANGUAGE SUPPORT

# I. FOCUS ON READING

## Focus on Skills

### Develop Visual Literacy

**OBJECTIVE:** Identify cause and effect

Explain to students that a cause is what makes something happen. The thing that happens is the effect. Demonstrate by pushing a chair over. Ask: *What happened?* (the chair fell over) *What caused the chair to fall over?* (The chair was pushed). Have students look at the photograph *Tractored Out, Childress County, Texas.* Ask them if they think anyone lives there. *Why not?* (The house looks empty and abandoned. There are no crops on the field) Ask students to think about what may have caused the crops to die. (No rain, high heat, insects).

**TPR**
Students can act out the scene they are presenting.

Lead students to understand that the lack of crops may have caused the farmers to move away. Then invite students to pair up and look through magazines and choose a photograph that shows the effect of a past incident. For example, they may see a photograph of a baby smiling while holding a balloon. The cause of her happiness could be that someone just gave her the balloon. Have students present their photographs, explaining both the cause and the effect implied within them. Return to the painting and ask students the following cause and effect related questions: *How does the ground look in the painting?* (it's in rows) What made the rows? (a tractor) *Why are there no crops?* (there was not enough rain and the crops died, the people moved away, and so on.)

# II. READ THE LITERATURE

### Vocabulary

**VOCABULARY**
county
clustered
sturdy
glistened
bidding
overflowing

Write the vocabulary words on the board and then read the sentences on Teacher Chart 44. Emphasize the vocabulary word and repeat the underlined context clues. Ask volunteers to act out or pantomime the context clues. For example, students can group together to form a crowd of people clustered. Invite students to suggest definitions and use them to replace the vocabulary words in the sentences. Have students check to see if the new definition fits with the underlined context clues. To check comprehension ask the following questions: *Which is bigger, a <u>county</u> or a state? Do you live in a county? If so, what is the name of your county? What is the name of your state? If you saw puppies <u>clustered</u> around a food bowl, would there be a few puppies or a bunch of puppies? Pretend that you built a <u>sturdy</u> treehouse. Would that treehouse be easy to knock down or hard to knock down? There are two cars. One is covered in mud and the other has just been washed. Which car <u>glistened</u> in the sun? The auctioneer started the <u>bidding</u> on the horse at $100. Is the auctioneer keeping the horse or is he selling the horse? If the sink was <u>overflowing</u>, would it be too full or too empty?*

Allow students to pose their own questions that use the vocabulary words. Students can pair up and answer each other's questions.

## CONCEPT

helping each other

nonverbal prompt for active participation

one- or two-word response prompt

prompt for short answers to higher-level thinking skills

prompt for detailed answers to higher-level thinking skills

### Evaluate Prior Knowledge

Dramatize the concept of helping each other by doing things around the classroom that are helpful. For example, help a student put on her or his coat, or tie her or his shoe; help a student with a math problem; offer a tissue to someone who has a cold. As students watch and listen, ask them what you are doing. Repeat with numerous examples until students understand that you are doing things to help others. Then provide magazines, and invite students to find photos which show people helping each other.

### Develop Oral Language

Invite students to talk about someone they know at home or at school who is helpful to other people. They may wish to work individually, in pairs, or in small groups.

- Preproduction: *Show us* (Point to class and self.) *what this person does to help others.*

- Early production: *What is this person's name? How do you know this person?*

- Speech emergence: *What does the person do to help others? What have you learned from this person?*

- Intermediate fluency: *How do you feel about helping others? How do you think it makes other people feel? What can you do to help other people?*

# Guided Instruction

### Preview and Predict

Tell students that in this story a young girl named Leah learns about the kindness of helpful people when her parents almost lose their farm. Ask students: *How do you think other people might help Leah and her family?* Write students' predictions. Then look through the story's illustrations with students, stopping to ask questions such as: *Why do you think Leah likes living on a farm? How can you tell? How does the land seem to change? How do you think that will affect Leah's family's farm? How do you think Leah will help her parents?*

**GRAPHIC ORGANIZER**
Blackline Master 29

### Objectives
- To identify cause and effect
- To develop critical thinking
- To understand sequence of events in a story

### Materials

One copy of Blackline Master 29 per student; pencils

Explain to students that in this story there are causes—why things happen—and effects—what happens. As students read, have them write or draw things that happen in the *Effect* column and then look for and write or draw the causes of these events in the *Cause* column. Encourage students to use the illustrations as well as the text to understand what has happened. Have students compare their findings when they finish.

To further reinforce cause and effect, have students work in pairs. Have each student write three effects (things that happen) and then switch worksheets with a partner to complete each other's *Cause* column (why those things happened).

# III. BUILD SKILLS

## Comprehension

**REVIEW CAUSE AND EFFECT**
Blackline Master 30

### Objectives
- To identify and explain relationships
- To use critical thinking
- To develop word identification skills

### Materials
One copy of Blackline Master 30 per student; pencils

Have students look over the *Cause and Effect* chart. Then remind them that in *Leah's Pony*, one thing causes another thing to happen. If necessary, read aloud the sentences and listed words with students. Have students use one of the listed words to fill in each sentence on the chart.

**INFORMAL ASSESSMENT**

To assess students' understanding of cause and effect, turn their attention to page 196. Have them read the first paragraph. Ask students what causes Leah's house to become very quiet. (The corn did not grow.) Then have them read the second paragraph. Ask what effect the hard wind has on life at the farm. (The sky turns black with dust; Leah can't keep her pony clean; Mama can't keep the house clean; it's hard for Papa to work.)

## Comprehension

**REVIEW SEQUENCE OF EVENTS**
Blackline Master 31

### Objectives
- To understand sequence of events
- To practice following directions
- To support hands-on learning

### Materials
One copy of Blackline Master 31 per student; pencils; oak tag; scissors; paste or glue

Tell students they will be making a "film" presentation of *Leah's Pony*. Ask students to review the events in the story to help them remember the order of events. Provide each student with a piece of oak tag and scissors, a strip of oak tag 15" long and 1-1/2" wide, and extra paper. Tell students to trace around the pictures below twice on the extra paper to make two blank squares. Have students cut out the squares and label one *Leah's Pony* and the other *The End*. On the strip of oak tag, have them paste the squares on opposite ends, with *The End* on the right. Then cut out and paste the large box from the worksheet onto a piece of oak tag. Have students cut out and arrange the pictures of the events from the story. Paste all the squares next to each other in the correct order on the oak tag strip. Help students cut out the dotted lines in the large square and thread their filmstrips through. Invite students to compare "films" to see if they recall the events in the same order.

**INFORMAL ASSESSMENT**

Turn to the illustration on pages 204 and 205, and ask students what Leah is doing here. (She is selling her pony.) Ask: *What happened before this?* (Leah's father told her about the auction.) *What happens next?* (Leah buys her father's tractor.)

# Vocabulary Strategy

## Objectives

• To identify context clues and help determine the meanings of unfamiliar words
• To increase vocabulary
• To understand simple sentences

## Materials

One copy of Blackline Master 32 per student; pencils

Remind students that the meaning of an unfamiliar word can sometimes be learned by the words and pictures surrounding it. Have students read the incomplete story and then fill in each blank with the appropriate word provided on the page. If necessary, read aloud the story and listed words.

**INFORMAL ASSESSMENT**  Turn to the text on page 199, and point out the word *borrowed*. Then help students read aloud through the words, *Papa paused.*" Ask students: *What information helps us understand what it means to borrow money?* (Papa says he cannot pay it back, which means he was supposed to.)

Name_____ Date_____

# Cause and Effect

| Cause (Why it Happens) | Effect (What Happens) |
|---|---|
| | |

# What Happened on the Farm

**1.** Fill in the blanks in the chart using the words shown below.

| rains | auctioned | saved | sold | lose | crops | money |
|-------|-----------|-------|------|------|-------|-------|

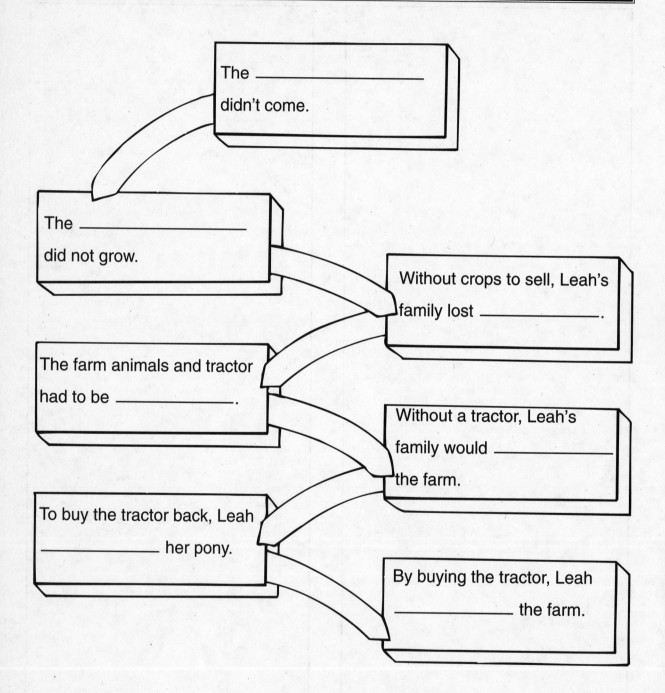

The _____ didn't come.

The _____ did not grow.

Without crops to sell, Leah's family lost _____.

The farm animals and tractor had to be _____.

Without a tractor, Leah's family would _____ the farm.

To buy the tractor back, Leah _____ her pony.

By buying the tractor, Leah _____ the farm.

# Make a Movie

# Finish the Story

**1.** Read the story. **2.** Use the words below to fill in the blanks.

| | | | |
|---|---|---|---|
| tractor | cornfield | pasture | cultivate |

Leah and her family live on a . On their farm,  grows

in a big open space called a _____. Leah's father has a Farmall

_____ that he uses for most of the important work on the farm.

He uses it to pull machines that _____, or get the soil ready for

planting.

On the farm, Leah's family also raises  and . The

 spend every day out in the _____ eating grass.

Leah's favorite animal, her , nibbles grass there, too.

# BASEBALL SAVED US pp. 216A–241P

Written by Ken Mochizuki  Illustrated by Dom Lee

## BUILD BACKGROUND FOR LANGUAGE SUPPORT

## I. FOCUS ON READING

### Focus on Skills

**OBJECTIVE:** Make predictions

**TPR**
Students making predictions can dramatize what they think will happen.

### Develop Visual Literacy

Say the following to students: *What will happen if you don't study for a test? Will you do well or badly? What will happen if you come home late? Will your mother be happy or mad? What will happen if you miss soccer practice? Will you play well or badly?* Explain that each time they answer questions such as these, they are making predictions about what will happen in the future. Turn students' attention to *The Rowers*, by Manuel Losada. Ask students to point to all the boats they see. In particular, help students notice the team of rowers in the background, as well as the one in the foreground. Then ask: *Which boat will win? Why? What do you think the winners will do after the race? How will they feel? What do you think the losers will do? How will they feel?* Then pair up native English speakers with those needing additional language support. Have students look through magazines for pictures of sporting events or other actions in progress. Encourage students to tell or act out what they think will happen. Alternatively, invite students to draw pictures of scenes from their own favorite sporting events. Ask them to include something that will make the viewers want to guess what will happen next. For instance, a student may draw a soccer player about to take a shot on goal, with a player from the other team about to side-tackle her or him. Have students present their pictures to the class and let classmates predict what will happen.

## II. READ THE LITERATURE

### Vocabulary

**VOCABULARY**
endless
ditches
crate
mound
glinting
inning

Introduce the vocabulary words by reading aloud the sentences on Teacher Chart 50. Emphasize the vocabulary word and repeat the underlined context clues. Invite students to suggest definitions and use their definition to replace the vocabulary word in each sentence. To check if the new definition fits the underlined context clues play a game of vocabulary baseball. Organize the class into two teams. Have the "batter" from one team step up. "Pitch" a word, and ask the batter to provide a definition. If the batter is right, her or his team gets a point. Then bring up the "batter" from the opposing team. Play until all vocabulary words are defined correctly. When the game is finished, have students use the vocabulary words in sentences of their own for review.

### Evaluate Prior Knowledge

**CONCEPT**
team spirit

Bring in sports photographs showing teammates working together to achieve a goal. Also show photographs of teams celebrating a victory or consoling each other after a defeat. Ask students what these photos have in common. Continue prompting until they see that these people are working as a team. Ask students: *Where else do you see people working together to get something done?* Help students think of other kinds of teams, such as firefighters, construction crews, doctors and nurses, neighbors working to keep their communities safe, and so on.

Students use body language and gestures to demonstrate their understanding of team spirit.

nonverbal prompt for active participation

one- or two-word response prompt

prompt for short answers to higher-level thinking skills

prompt for detailed answers to higher-level thinking skills

## Develop Oral Language

Invite students to work in small groups to create skits about team spirit. Remind them that team spirit is not about having one star player, but about everyone working together.

• Preproduction: *Show us* (point to class and self) *what your team does together.*

• Early production: *Do you like working as a team? Is it easier to work as a team than alone?*

• Speech emergence: *What is your team doing? What do each of you do to help your team?*

• Intermediate fluency: *How do you feel about working as a team? Why is it easier than trying to do something alone?*

## Guided Instruction

### Preview and Predict

Tell students that this story is based on real historical events. Turn to the title page, and have a volunteer read aloud the title. Ask students: *What do you think this story is about? What can you tell about the children in the picture?* After listening to students' answers, explain that during World War II, many Japanese Americans were forced to live in government camps. With this information, ask students how they think baseball may have "saved" the young boy in the illustration. Also, ask students who they think the "us" in the story title refers to. Then guide students through the story's illustrations, allowing them time to observe the setting and events. Ask students questions such as: *How do you think the boy feels about being in the camp? How do you think the young boy feels when he is part of a team? What do you think this boy will learn from being in the camps and from being part of a team?*

**GRAPHIC ORGANIZER**
Blackline Master 33

### Objectives

• To practice making predictions
• To encourage creative thinking
• To practice summarizing events

### Materials

One copy of Blackline Master 33 per student; pencils

Explain to students that information at the beginning of a story can help the reader predict, or guess, what will happen next. As students begin to read *Baseball Saved Us*, invite them to write their predictions in the left column of the chart. Then have them write what really happens in the right column. If necessary, pair students needing language support with more fluent readers and writers. To help students begin, have them look again at the illustration on p. 219, and ask students to make a prediction about where the story takes place. Then as students read, have them look for evidence from the text to support or refute their prediction. Then, students can fill in the *What Happened* column with this information.

As an alternate way to reinforce predictions, organize the class into two groups. Have each group write a prediction about the story. Then tell them to trade charts. Each group will search to find what really happens in relation to the other group's prediction.

# III. BUILD SKILLS

## Comprehension

### REVIEW MAKE PREDICTIONS
Blackline Master 34

**Objectives**
- To use story clues to make predictions
- To practice following directions
- To practice reading skills

**Materials**

One copy of Blackline Master 34 per student; pencils

Help students read the sentences that describe events from the story. Then ask them to circle the letter of the statement that best matches their prediction of what will happen next. Next, have students look back at the story to compare what really happened with what they predicted would happen. Have students mark their correct answers on the scoreboard.

**INFORMAL ASSESSMENT**

To assess students' skills at making reasonable predictions, turn to the illustration on pages 220–221, and ask students what they think the father is planning to do. (make a baseball field) Repeat the exercise on pages 230–231, asking what they think will happen between the boy and the guard. (The boy hits the ball very far, and the guard congratulates him.) Ask students to identify the clues in the text and illustrations which led them to make their predictions.

## Comprehension

### REVIEW FORM GENERALIZATIONS
Blackline Master 35

**Objectives**
- To form generalizations based on details and clues
- To develop critical thinking
- To support hands-on learning

**Materials**

One copy of Blackline Master 35 per student; crayons

Explain to students that generalizations are general ideas that people form from a few specific experiences. Tell students that sometimes people make false generalizations based on a few experiences. These generalizations may lead to false beliefs. For example, people used to believe the world was flat because in their experience, it appeared to drop off at the horizon. In their experience, they did not believe the world was round. Help students read each sentence on the worksheet. Explain that some of these statements are false generalizations made by people in the story. Ask students to color in the baseball icons that are next to the false generalizations. If necessary, read sentences aloud with students.

**INFORMAL ASSESSMENT**

To assess students' recognition of false generalizations, turn to the text on page 232. Help students read the paragraph aloud, and then ask: *What false generalization might the other kids be making about the young boy?* (Japanese are not to be trusted or made friends with.) Repeat the exercise on page 236, asking students what generalization the crowd makes. (The Japanese boy is not good at baseball.) Remind students that these generalizations are false beliefs.

# Vocabulary Strategy

## COMPOUND WORDS
Blackline Master 36

### Objectives
• To recognize and figure out the meaning of compound words
• To increase vocabulary
• To practice following directions

### Materials

One copy of Blackline Master 36 per student; scissors; paste or glue; pencils

Remind students that compound words are words formed when two smaller words are joined together. Explain that the word on the pitcher's mound of each baseball diamond can be combined with the words on the bases to make several compound words. Tell students they will see how many compound words they can make. Have students cut out the words at the bottom of the page. Have them place each word on the base of a diamond to form a new word. Invite students to write the compound words they have made below each diamond.

### INFORMAL ASSESSMENT

To assess students' understanding of compound words, turn their attention to the text on page 224, and point to the word *bathroom*. Ask volunteers to explain what two words make up this compound word. (*bath* and *room*) Invite them to share how the two original words help explain the meaning of the compound word. Repeat the exercise on page 230 with the word *guardhouse*.

# Make Predictions

| Predictions | What Happens |
|---|---|
| | |

# What's Your Score?

**1.** Read the sentences below that describe events from the story, *How Baseball Saved Us*. **2.** Circle the letter of what you think happened. **3.** Look back at the story to compare what really happened with what you thought happened. **4.** Keep score of your correct guesses on the scoreboard.

**1.** When the people in the camp start making a baseball diamond, the guards will:

a. make them stop
b. watch their every move
c. help them
d. throw things at them

**2.** When the boy in the story comes up to bat in the championship game, he will:

a. strike out
b. run away
c. hit a home run
d. start joking around

**3.** When the boy gets back home, other kids will:

a. welcome him
b. ignore him
c. beat him up
d. help him

**4.** When the boy plays baseball back home, he will:

a. be a failure
b. get sick
c. get thrown out
d. hit another home run

## Scoreboard

| My Prediction | What Happens |
|---|---|
| 1. | 1. |
| 2. | 2. |
| 3. | 3. |
| 4. | 4. |

# Not All, Not Always

Color the baseballs next to the sentences that are generalizations in the story, *Baseball Saved Us*.

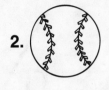 1. All good baseball players are tall.

 2. All the camp guards were mean to the prisoners.

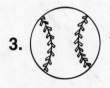 3. The United States was at war with Japan.

 4. The camp guard was rooting for the boy in the story when he stepped up to bat.

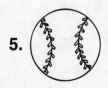 5. The small boy in the story hit a home run.

Name_____ Date_____

# Bases Loaded!

**1.** In the center of each baseball diamond is a word that can be put together with the words below to make several compound words. **2.** See how many different compound words you can make. **3.** Cut out the bases and paste each one on a base in the base-ball diamonds. **4.** Write the compound words on the lines below the baseball diamonds.

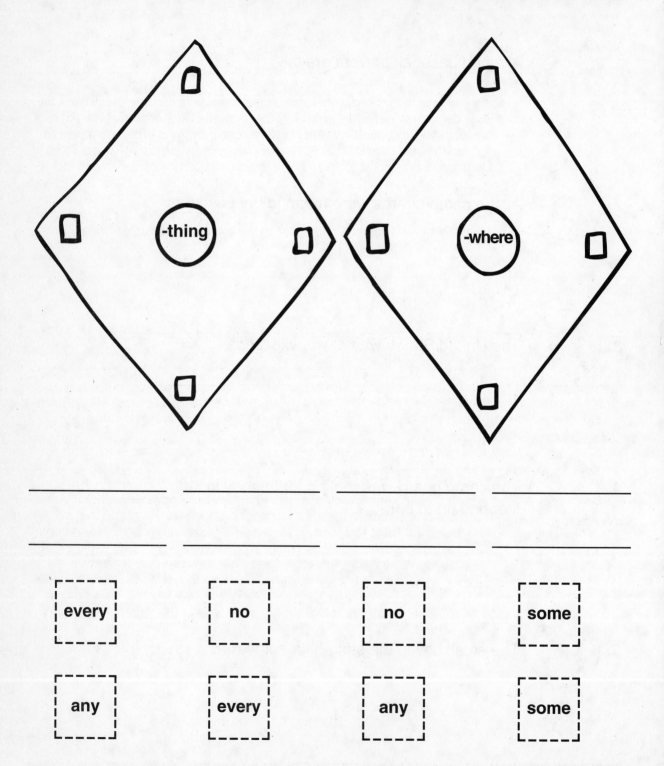

_____ _____   _____ _____

_____ _____   _____ _____

| every | no | no | some |

| any | every | any | some |

# WILL HER NATIVE LANGUAGE DISAPPEAR? pp. 282A–297P

Time For Kids

## BUILD BACKGROUND FOR LANGUAGE SUPPORT

## I. FOCUS ON READING

**Focus on Skills**

**OBJECTIVE:** Identify cause
and effect

**TPR**
Students can use body language to explain the reasons
something has become extinct
or endangered.

### Develop Visual Literacy

Review cause and effect with students. Then direct students' attention to the painting *Workers Dragging Building Blocks*. Invite students to gather in a line like the people in the picture. Ask students: *What are the workers trying to do? What effect does standing in a line have on their movement?* Guide students to see that by standing in a line and pulling together, the workers are able to drag the block. Then ask: *What do you think they might build with that block? Tell them that there is writing in this painting, and then ask them to find it.* Point out the hieroglyphics and explain that it is a form of picture-writing used by the ancient Egyptians. Ask students: *What effect does the writing have on you?* Guide students to see that because they don't know the meaning of the hieroglyphics, they cannot understand the meaning of the writing. Encourage students to guess what the writing says. Challenge students to write a message using drawings. Invite them to trade "hieroglyphics" with a partner and guess what each message might say.

## II. READ THE LITERATURE

**VOCABULARY**
century
generations
communicate
extinct
backgrounds
native

### Vocabulary

Write the vocabulary words on the chalkboard. Introduce the words by reading the sentences from Teaching Chart 56. Emphasize the vocabulary word in each sentence and invite students to identify the underlined context clues. Write the context clues on the chalkboard. Lead students in a matching game with the context clues and corresponding vocabulary words. After each successful match, invite students to guess the word's definition. Decide as a class the correct definition. Then have students get together in small groups and write sentences using each of the vocabulary words. Suggest that the groups present each sentence with an accompanying role-play.

### Evaluate Prior Knowledge

**CONCEPT**
Native American cultures

Bring in photographs and books showing diverse, authentic Native American cultures from all over North America. Show a map of North America. Point to the map and explain that Native Americans were living in this country long before European explorers, like Christopher Columbus, came to America. Encourage students to share what they know about Native American cultures. Write their ideas on the chalkboard. Encourage students to use the photographs and books to brainstorm the different types of food, shelter, and activities that are part of Native American culture. (corn, buffalo, canoes, nature, pottery, drums, and so on) Ask, *What does the name Native American mean?*

Grade 4                                            **Will Her Native Language Disappear? 73**

## Develop Oral Language

Invite students to act out scenes from the photographs of different Native American cultures or from prior knowledge. Students may wish to work individually or in small groups. Make sure students portray Native American cultures as they are today as well as how they once were.

• Preproduction: *Show us* (point to class and self) *an activity that is special to a Native American culture.*

• Early production: *Did you know about Native American cultures before today? Do you enjoy learning about Native Americans?*

• Speech emergence: *What is your activity called? Who usually does it? What does the activity involve? Would you enjoy it? Why or why not?*

• Intermediate fluency: *Why is (name activity) important? What is involved in* (name activity)*? Who might have participated in this activity? What would be hard about it? What would be easy?*

# Guidelced Instruction

## Preview and Predict

Tell students that this selection is a true story about a Native American man who is working hard to keep his native language alive. Ask students: *Why do you think his language may disappear?* Write their predictions and ask them to check their answers after reading the selection. Use the photographs in the selection to prompt more predictions from students. For instance, ask a volunteer to read aloud the selection and predict how the young girl's life may be affected if her native language disappears. Next, ask: *Where do you think the story takes place? What do you think the man and the little girl are doing? Why?* Turn students' attention to the photograph of the turtle and remind them of what the story is about. Then ask: *Why do you think there is a photograph of a turtle here?* Finally, point to the picture writing and ask students to name the pictures shown. Ask: *How do you think these images might be related to Native American culture? How do you think they were used by Native Americans?* Finally, ask students to predict what would happen if the Choctaw language disappeared. Ask, *How do you think people may try to stop it from disappearing?*

## Objectives

• To identify cause and effect
• To use critical thinking

## Materials

One copy of Blackline Master 37 per student; pencils

As students read the selection, have them record what happens in a *Cause and Effect* chart. Tell students to write or draw illustrations to represent things that happen in the selection in the *Effect* column and the events or situations which caused those things to happen in the *Cause* column. In addition, have students write about what could happen in the future of the Choctaw language and the possible causes and effects.

# III. BUILD SKILLS

## Comprehension

**REVIEW FACT AND OPINION**
Blackline Master 38

**Objectives**
• To identify and form generalizations
• To encourage critical thinking

**Materials**
One copy of Blackline Master 38 per student; pencils

Remind students that generalizations are ideas about people, places, or things that can be made from putting pieces of information together. Explain that words like *many, most, few, everyone,* and *usually* are clues to identifying generalizations. Then have students review the two pictures on the worksheet. Explain that both pictures show something that is endangered. Then ask students to make a generalization about what the falcon and the language have in common that makes them endangered and write it on the lines provided. Student answers will vary.

**INFORMAL ASSESSMENT**

To assess students' recognition of generalizations, turn their attention to the two captions on page 245. Help them read the captions. Ask: *Which statement is a generalization?* (Most Choctaws live in Oklahoma.)

## Vocabulary Strategy

**REVIEW SUMMARIZING**
Blackline Master 39

**Objectives**
• To identify compound words
• To use structural clues to determine the meaning of compound words

**Materials**
One copy of Blackline Master 39 per pair of students; scissors; timer

Remind students that compound words are made from two smaller words that are joined together to make a new one. Help students read aloud the words on their worksheets. Organize the class into groups of four, each group in turn divided into teams of two. Have the teams cut out the half-shells on the worksheet, turn them face down, and mix them up. Tell each team they will have five minutes to turn the pieces face up and put pairs of words together to form new, compound words. Set the timer and say "go" when everyone is ready. The first team to put all the words together in each group wins.

**INFORMAL ASSESSMENT**

Turn students' attention to the first sentence at the top of page 246. Point out the words animal and wildlife and ask students which one is a compound word. (wildlife) Have students explain their thinking. (It comes from the words wild and life.) Repeat the exercise with the sentence at the top of page 247, using the words sometimes and believes.

# Vocabulary Strategy

## Objectives

- To identify context clues
- To use context clues to understand specialized vocabulary

## Materials

One copy of Blackline Master 40 per student; crayons

Allow students time to review the Choctaw vocabulary shown on page 246. If appropriate, have students practice saying the words and phrases with partners. Then ask them to put the selection away and turn to their worksheets. Explain that each English word in the right column describes the meaning of one of the Choctaw words in the left column. Have students match the English words with their corresponding Choctaw words by drawing lines between them.

**INFORMAL ASSESSMENT**

To assess students' understanding of Choctaw words, cover up the English words on the chart on page 246 and ask volunteers to say the Choctaw word as well as its English translation. If students have a hard time, you may wish to offer clues either through body language or by saying the Choctaw words in English sentences, such as "Halito, how are you today?"

# Cause and Effect

| Cause | Effect |
|-------|--------|

| Why Something Happens | What Happens |
|------------------------|--------------|
| _____ | _____ |
| _____ | _____ |
| _____ | _____ |
| _____ | _____ |
| _____ | _____ |
| _____ | _____ |
| _____ | _____ |
| _____ | _____ |
| _____ | _____ |
| _____ | _____ |

# Going, Going, Gone

**1.** Look at the two pictures. Each shows something that is endangered. One is an animal, and one is a human language. **2.** On the lines write what the bird and the language have in common that makes them both endangered.

The falcon is endangered because

_____ _____

_____

_____ .

The Choctaw language is endangered

because _____

_____

_____ .

# Compound Word Shell Game

**1.** Look at the pictures below. **2.** Find words that you can put together to form compound words. **3.** Write the compound words on the lines below.

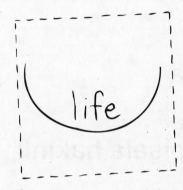
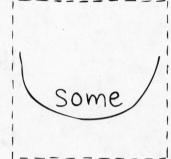

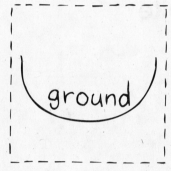

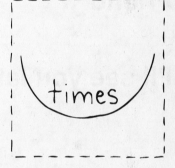

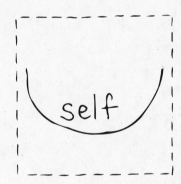
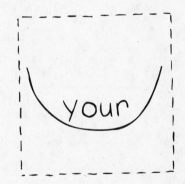

_____          _____

_____          _____

# Speaking Choctaw

1. Look at the words in each group below. 2. The English words describe the meaning of the Choctaw words. 3. Draw a line connecting the correct English words with Choctaw words.

Thank you                    Ikana

Hello                        Chi pisala hakinli

Friend                       Yakoke

I'll see you later           Halito

# THE HATMAKER'S SIGN pp. 156A–281P

Retold by Candace Fleming   Illustrated by Robert Andrew Parker

## BUILD BACKGROUND FOR LANGUAGE SUPPORT

## I. FOCUS ON READING

### Focus on Skills

**OBJECTIVE:** Make judgments and decisions

**TPR**

### Develop Visual Literacy

Ask students to draw pictures of things they have in their refrigerator. Then ask them to draw foods they like. Ask the class to name the place where these items can be found. Have students then turn to the painting *Food City*, by Richard Estes. Ask them if these items might be found at a place such as Food City. Ask them to describe the details of the scene and to pretend that they are actually standing in front of the store window, about to enter the store. Ask: *Do the signs tell us about the things in the store? Would you buy something from this store? Why?* Lead students to see that some items are sold for less than others, and that may affect what they decide to buy. Then have students work in small groups to create their own grocery store display. Ask two groups of volunteers to come to the front of the room and pretend they are in the scene in *Food City*. Have one cashier, one customer and one person to bag the groceries.

## II. READ THE LITERATURE

### Vocabulary

**VOCABULARY**
strolling
wharf
admitted
elegantly
brisk
displaying

Bring in photographs of an elegantly dressed person and a picture of a wharf. Print each vocabulary word on a flashcard. Point to the flashcard for a word as you say it aloud and read the corresponding sentences from Teacher Chart 62. As you read the sentences for *strolling*, walk leisurely across the classroom stopping briefly to point to the flashcard. As you read the word *admitted* in the sentence nod your head up and down to indicate admission. As you read *displaying* use arm as if to reveal an object. And for *brisk* rub left arm with right hand and right arm with left hand to indicate chilly weather. Then have students turn back to the Visual Literacy painting *Food City*, by Richard Estes and ask the following: *If you were strolling by this window, would you be walking or in a car? What would you buy in this store? If you wanted to buy fresh fish, would you go to the wharf? What other things would you see at the wharf? If the store manager admitted that his prices were too high, would that be the truth or a lie? Do you think people inside the store are dressed elegantly? Where would you see people who are dressed elegantly? Pretend that it is windy outside the store. Would a brisk breeze be cool or warm? What type of food is the store displaying in the windows? What else is the store displaying in the windows?*

Line the flashcards up on the chalkboard ledge in random order. Repeat the sentences, this time leaving out the vocabulary word. Ask pairs of students to come forward to select the correct flashcard.

## Evaluate Prior Knowledge

Bring in a copy of the Declaration of Independence, photographs of historical sites of the American Revolution, portraits of its leaders, and a map showing the thirteen colonies. Ask students if the places and people portrayed are from today or long ago. Then invite students to compare the thirteen colonies with the United States as it is today. Explain to students: *The people in the portraits helped free the United States from the British Empire, which was not treating them well. This war was called the American Revolution. The Declaration of Independence was a piece of writing that said the United States was now independent of, or free from, the rule of the British Empire.* Guide students in a dramatization of a scene from the Revolution, such as the signing of the Declaration of Independence.

## Develop Oral Language

Invite students to create dioramas showing scenes from the American Revolution that are represented in the photographs you have displayed, such as the Boston Tea Party, Paul Revere's ride, or the signing of the Declaration of Independence.

- Preproduction: *Show us* (point to class and self) *the scene from the American Revolution you have created.*

- Early production: *Did this scene help the American Revolution? Did it involve one person or many?*

- Speech emergence: *What is your scene called? Who was involved? Where did it take place?*

- Intermediate fluency: *How did your scene help the American Revolution? How would you have felt if you had been a part of this scene during the American Revolution?*

# Guided Instruction

## Preview and Predict

Tell students that this selection tells two stories, one inside the other. Say: *The first story is about Thomas Jefferson writing the Declaration of Independence and how sad he was that people wanted to change the words. The second story is one that his friend Ben Franklin tells to help him feel better.* Then have a volunteer read aloud the selection's title, and ask the class what they think Ben Franklin's story will be about. Write their predictions on the board, and invite students to guess how the two stories are related. Next, guide students through the illustrations in the book, and encourage them to predict what the hatmaker is trying to do, judging by the selection's title. Pause at each page that shows how the sign has been changed. Ask students: *If the hatmaker's sign is getting smaller and smaller, what do you think might also be happening to the Declaration of Independence?* As you go along, invite students to note the setting and the characters in the story and to make the connection that this story takes place during the American Revolution.

## Objectives

- To develop understanding of judgments and decisions
- To organize information

**Materials**

One copy of Blackline Master 41 per student; pencils

Explain to students that in this story many judgments and decisions are made. Have them use the *Judgments and Decisions* chart to note both the judgments and decisions that are made (left column) and the things in the story that support those decisions (right column). When students are finished, have them compare their findings with those of the rest of the class. If necessary, model how to fill in the chart with the first judgment and decision, beginning with how Thomas Jefferson feels about this writing.

For a different approach to reviewing judgments and decisions, organize students into small groups. Have members of each group take turns naming a decision or judgment made within the story, while the rest of the group tries to find and write the supporting evidence.

# III. BUILD SKILLS

## Comprehension

**REVIEW MAKE JUDG-MENTS AND DECISIONS**
Blackline Master 42

**Objectives**
• To develop critical thinking
• To practice making judgments and decisions

**Materials**
One copy of Blackline Master 42 per student; pencils

Tell students that people in different professions, or kinds of work, tend to wear different kinds of hats to suit their needs. Ask them to name different kinds of hats with which they are familiar (hard hats, baseball caps, firefighter helmets). Write these on the board. Then have students look at the hats on the worksheet and use their best judgment to decide and write what kind of hat each one is.

**INFORMAL ASSESSMENT**

To assess students' ability to make judgments and decisions, turn to the illustrations on pages 269, 270, and 273, and ask them to share their thoughts on why the different people shown decide to wear different kinds of hats. (Answers may vary. For example: The woman wears a bonnet to match her dress; The magistrate wears a hat that makes him look tough; The professor wears a hat to keep the sun out of his eyes.) On page 275, ask why the hatmaker holds his hat in his hand and the sign-maker wears no hat at all. (It is polite to take your hat off inside.)

## Comprehension

**INTRODUCE SUMMARIZE**
Blackline Master 43

**Objectives**
• To develop understanding of summarizing
• To practice following directions
• To practice reading skills

**Materials**
One copy of Blackline Master 43 per student; scissors; paste or glue

Explain to students that when people summarize, they tell only the most important parts of a story. Have students look over the pictures on the worksheet, which summarize *The Hatmaker's Sign*. Invite them to complete the summary by cutting out the three pictures at the bottom of the page and pasting them in the appropriate boxes. Then have students use the pictures as aids to help them summarize the story in their own words.

**INFORMAL ASSESSMENT**

To assess students' ability to summarize, turn to the illustration on pages 274–275, and ask them to summarize what is happening. (The signmaker is designing the hatmaker's sign.) Then turn to the following two pages and repeat the exercise, asking students to summarize this scene. (Everyone agrees that the wording of the Declaration of Independence is fine as is.)

## Vocabulary Strategy

**INTRODUCE SUFFIX -FUL**
Blackline Master 44

### Objectives

• To develop knowledge of suffix -ful
• To increase vocabulary
• To practice critical thinking

### Materials

One copy of Blackline Master 44 per student; pencils

Explain to students that adding the suffix -ful to the end of a word gives it a slightly different meaning. Have them add this suffix to the end of each word listed and say the new word aloud. Then ask them to choose and write the word that best describes each picture. If necessary, go over the pictures with students.

**INFORMAL ASSESSMENT**

Turn to the text on page 261, and ask students to find the word containing the suffix -ful. (wonderful) Invite students to explain how this word was made from another word and the suffix. (wonder and -ful) Have them use the word in a sentence of their own. You may wish to repeat the exercise with the word unlawful on page 270, though you will need to discuss the prefix un- as well.

# Make Judgments and Decisions

| Judgments and Decisions | Evidence from the Story |
|---|---|
|  |  |

# Hats Off to You!

**1.** Look at the hats below. **2.** Describe each hat. **3.** What kind of hat would you like to wear?

B

# Tell Me a Story

**1.** Cut out the three squares at the bottom of the page. **2.** Paste them where they belong in the squares below.

**John Thompson Hatmaker Fashionable Hats Sold Inside for Ready Money**

**Fashionable Hats Sold Inside**

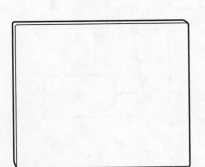

**Hats**

**John Thompson Hatmaker Fashionable Hats Sold Inside for Ready Money**

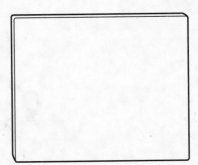

**John Thompson Hatmaker Fashionable Hats Sold Inside**

**Hats Sold Inside**

# Full Time

**1.** Write the suffix **-ful** at the end of each word below. **2.** Use one of the words to best describe each picture below.

| wonder | help | thank | care |
|--------|------|-------|------|

_____

_____

_____

_____

# PAT CUMMINGS: MY STORY pp. 282A–297P

Written and Illustrated by Pat Cummings

## BUILD BACKGROUND FOR LANGUAGE SUPPORT

## I. FOCUS ON READING

### Focus on Skills

**OBJECTIVE:** Distinguish between fact and opinion

**TPR**
Students can use body language and facial expressions to help express their opinions.

### Develop Visual Literacy

Review fact and opinion with students. Have students look at the painting *Blue Dancers,* by Edgar Degas. On the left side of the chalkboard write the name of the painting and the painter. Say: *Edgar Degas painted this painting. I think this is his best painting.* Explain that the first statement is a fact because it can be proven. The second statement is an opinion because it tells about feelings and ideas. Ask students: *Who are the women in the painting?* Write students responses on the chalkboard. Then ask students to share how they feel about both the painting and the painter. Ask: *Do you think Degas was a good painter? Do you think the painting is well done? Why or why not?* Write students' opinions on the right side of the board. Help students decide which is fact and which is opinion. Finally, have students create their own paintings and share facts and opinions about each other's work.

## II. READ THE LITERATURE

### Vocabulary

**VOCABULARY**
exist
image
reference
sketch
loft
inspire

Print each vocabulary word on a flashcard. Display the flashcard for a word as you say it aloud and read the corresponding sentences from Teacher Chart 68. Then have students take turns guessing at definitions for each word. Write their suggestions on the board. Then ask volunteers to repeat the sentences, using the suggested definitions in place of the vocabulary words. Decide as a class which definition is correct for each word. Then have students form small groups and give each group a flashcard. Have students work together writing a sentence using the vocabulary word.

### Evaluate Prior Knowledge

**CONCEPT**

children's art

Bring in samples of art designed for children, such as comic books, illustrated children's literature, newspaper comics, and picture books. Give students time to look through several sources and find a picture or pictures they like. Then ask volunteers to hold up a picture that they like for the rest of the class to see. Show students a picture book and ask: *Why are there no words in this book?* Explain that children who cannot read may be able to understand a story told in pictures. Ask students what all the different types of art have in common. Ask, *What do you like about this art? Who would enjoy looking at these pictures more: you or your parents? Would you read this book if there were no pictures?* Continue until the class concludes that the pictures are all examples of art for children.

### Develop Oral Language

Invite students to talk about someone they know at home or at school who is helpful to other people. They may wish to work individually, in pairs, or in small groups.

nonverbal prompt for active participation

- Preproduction: *Show us* (Point to class and self) *the art you chose. Do you like it?*

one- or two-word response prompt

- Early production: *Have you seen this art before? Do you like it? What is this?* (point to object in art)

prompt for short answers to higher-level thinking skills

- Speech emergence: *What art did you choose? Why did you choose it? What is in the picture? Have you seen art like this before? Where?*

prompt for detailed answers to higher-level thinking skills

- Intermediate fluency: *Tell us about the art? Why do you like this art? Do you think the artist is good? Why? If you were an artist, what would you paint or draw?*

## Guided Instruction

### Preview and Predict

Tell students that this selection is about the life and work of a children's book illustrator. Explain that Pat Cummings has been drawing for a very long time. Ask students: *What do you think Pat Cummings drew when she was a little girl? With what do you think she might have liked to draw? What other tools does she use in her work?* Write students' predictions. Then guide students page by page through the illustrations in the book. Point out the drawing of the ballerina and ask students why Pat Cummings may have drawn this picture when she was little. Looking at the pictures towards the end of the book, ask students if they see any common themes. Ask: *Why do you think Pat Cummings might like to draw these kinds of images? What kinds of stories do you think Pat Cummings might usually draw for?*

**GRAPHIC ORGANIZER**
Blackline Master 45

### Objectives

- To develop understanding of facts and opinions
- To practice spelling skills
- To reinforce critical thinking

### Materials

One copy of Blackline Master 45 per student; pencils

As students read the story, have them note facts about Pat Cummings' life and work in the left column of their worksheets. In the right column, ask students to write down any opinions they discover in the story. Remind students that facts are statements which can be proven, while opinions are feelings or ideas about something. You may want to have students work together to fill out their charts.

# III. BUILD SKILLS

## Comprehension

**REVIEW FACT AND OPINION**
Blackline Master 46

### Objectives
• To distinguish between fact and opinion
• To encourage creative thinking
• To use illustrations

### Materials
One copy of Blackline Master 46 per student; crayons; pencils

Remind students that a fact is something that can be proved true or false, while an opinion is what a person thinks. Add that an opinion is neither right nor wrong. Have students review the pictures on worksheet and circle the word that correctly completes each fact sentence. Then ask students to write in their own word to complete each opinion sentence.

**INFORMAL ASSESSMENT**

To assess students' recognition of facts and opinions, turn to page 287. Ask students to give one fact about the picture and one opinion about the picture. Then have students turn to page 290 and read the last paragraph. Have them identify one fact and one opinion.

## Comprehension

**REVIEW SUMMARIZING**
Blackline Master 47

### Objectives
• To summarize a selection
• To recall story events
• To practice critical thinking

### Materials
One copy of Blackline Master 47 per student; crayons

Explain to students that the illustrations in a story often help summarize, or tell the main parts of a story. Have students review the pictures on the worksheet. Then have them color in only the pictures that help summarize the story of Pat Cummings' life and work. When they are done coloring, invite them to use the illustrations to summarize the story in their own words.

**INFORMAL ASSESSMENT**

Turn to page 290. Help students read aloud the passage about Pat Cummings' cat. Then ask them to use both the text and the illustration to summarize this passage.

# Vocabulary Strategy

**REVIEW SUFFIXES**
Blackline Master 48

## Objectives

- To add suffixes to base words
- To understand new word meanings
- To practice following directions

## Materials

One copy of Blackline Master 48 per student; pencils

Remind students that new words can be created when a suffix, or ending, is added to an original word. Have students follow the mathematics directions to make new words. Have students write the new word on the line provided and then match that word to the picture it best describes.

**INFORMAL ASSESSMENT**

To assess students' understanding of suffixes, turn to the text on page 292 and point to the word *disastrous*. Ask a volunteer to take away the ending and add whatever letters are necessary to show the original word. (disaster)

# Fact and Opinion

| Facts | Opinions |
|-------|----------|
|       |          |

# I Think I See...

**1.** Circle the correct word that goes in the "Fact" sentence. **2.** Write a word to go in the "Opinion" blank.

Fact:

This is a _____.   mountain   cloud

Opinion:

I think this looks like a _____.

Fact:

This is a _____.   tree   river

Opinion:

I think this looks like a _____.

Fact:

This is a _____.   house   river

Opinion:

I think this looks like a _____.

Fact:

This is a _____.   rock   flower

Opinion:

I think this looks like a _____.

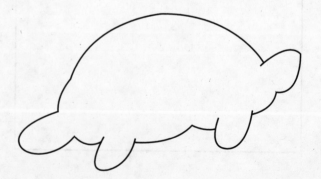

# That Reminds Me

**1.** Color the pictures that help you retell the story.

| | |
|---|---|
| CRAYONS | |
| | |
| | |
| | |

# Endings

**1.** Write each new word in the lines below. **2.** Choose a picture to go with each new word. **3.** Draw a line connecting the word to the picture it describes.

adventure – e + ous = _____

disaster – e + ous = _____

beauty – y + i + ful = _____

wonder + ful = _____

# GRASS SANDALS pp. 298A–331P

Written by Dawnine Spivak  Illustrated by Demi

## BUILD BACKGROUND FOR LANGUAGE SUPPORT

## I. FOCUS ON READING

### Focus on Skills

**OBJECTIVE:** Identify author's purpose and point of view

**TPR**
Have students dramatize the scene shown in the stained glass window. Other students can circle around the "models" and discuss how the scene looks from different points of view.

### Develop Visual Literacy

Point out to students the pilgrims journey in the scene from the stained glass window, *Pilgrims Going to Canterbury.* Ask students to point to colors in the stained glass window they like and name them. Ask students to point to objects in the window they recognize and name them (people, horse, sword). Ask students: *How many people do you see? Do you think they are cold or warm?* Say: *Pretend you are standing somewhere watching these people pass by. Where might you be?* (Answers may include: beside the road, in a field, in a small village, or in a farm house.) Finally, ask students to draw the scene from a different point of view. Ask them to show, for instance, what the scene would look like from the eyes of the person on horseback or from one of the people walking behind the horse. Invite students to share their different points of view and what the purpose of showing things from that angle might be (to show where the people are going or where they have been).

## II. READ THE LITERATURE

### Vocabulary

**VOCABULARY**
stitching
chanted
nipped
pouch
scribbled
restless

If possible bring to class the following props: a threaded needle, a pouch, a piece of fabric with a hole in it, a pencil and a piece of paper. Read the sentences on Teacher Chart 74 to introduce the words. Emphasize the vocabulary word and repeat the underlined context clues. Read the first sentence again. Using the props act out the sentence while repeating the sentence. Then read the sentence once more. Continue this way for each sentence. Ask volunteers to act out the sentence. Then have them act out the vocabulary words. Invite students to suggest definitions for each. Then write the vocabulary words on one side of the chalkboard. On the other side write the following fill-in-the-blank sentences. Have students work in small groups to guess which word finishes each sentence. Then have one person from each group come up and complete a sentence on the blackboard.

*Mom is _____ (stitching) the rip in my shirt with a needle and thread.*

*I _____ (chanted) the song over and over as I walked to school this morning.*

*The tiny flea _____ (nipped) me on the ankle!*

*I put my marbles in the _____ (pouch) to keep them safe.*

*She quickly _____ (scribbled) a message on her note pad.*

*The movie was so long and boring that I started to get _____ (restless).*

Encourage partners to share their work with other students.

**CONCEPT**
poets and poems

### Evaluate Prior Knowledge

Explain to students that poetry is a form of writing that expresses thoughts and emotions in a style that is different from ordinary writing. Read to the class *My Poems* by Alan Barlow on page 371. While reading use body language and facial expressions to convey the thoughts and emotions the poet was trying to communicate with the poem. Ask students to explain what they thought the poem was about.

**TPR**

Have students use body language and gestures to act out one of the poems you read.

nonverbal prompt for active participation

one- or two-word response prompt

prompt for short answers to higher-level thinking skills

prompt for detailed answers to higher-level thinking skills

### Develop Oral Language

Tell students to point to their nose, mouth, eyes, ears and hand. Ask them to explain what they do with each (smell, taste, see, hear and touch) Explain to students that these are the five senses. Then ask students (in small groups or individually) to create a poem about their senses.

• Preproduction: *Show us* (point to class and self) *what your poem is about. Show us how you feel* (point to student) *about your sense of* (point to student).

• Early production: *Is your poem a funny poem? Is it a sad poem? Is there a lot of action in your poem?*

• Speech emergence: *What is the name of your poem? What is the name of the person who wrote your poem? What is your poem about?*

• Intermediate fluency: *How does this poem make you feel? What do you like to write about?*

## Guided Instruction

### Preview and Predict

Tell students that this is a story about a real Japanese poet named Basho, who lived long, long ago. Explain to them that Basho traveled throughout Japan and wrote poems. Basho had the opportunity in his travels to see his country and meet his countrymen. Tell students that in the story they will see poetry in addition to the main story. Turn to page 301, and ask someone to read the title aloud. Ask: *Why do you think Basho travels? What do you think Basho might see in his travels?* Write students' predictions. Then point to the Japanese characters on page 300, and ask if anyone knows what these are. Establish that these characters represent words in Japanese and that they also tell about things Basho sees on his travels. Guide students through a picture walk of the story, stopping at each page that shows a Japanese character. Ask students to use the illustrations to predict what each character might mean. At each page, ask: *What do you think Basho might write poems about here?* Give students time to explain their predictions.

**GRAPHIC ORGANIZER**
Blackline Master 49

### Objectives

• To understand author's purpose
• To reinforce critical thinking
• To practice summarizing

## Materials

One copy of Blackline Master 49 per student; pencils

Remind students that authors often have a purpose, or reason, for writing a story. Ask students to review the selection and write in the right column what they think may be the author's purpose. In the left column, have them write the clues in the selection that support that purpose.

Alternatively, invite partners to help each other find clues that show what the author's purpose may have been for writing this story. Have each partner write down her or his idea of the author's purpose. Have the other partner search for and write the clues that support that purpose.

# III. BUILD SKILLS

## Comprehension

**REVIEW FACT AND OPINION**
Blackline Master 50

### Objectives
- To develop understanding of author's purpose and point of view
- To reinforce critical thinking
- To use illustrations
- To practice reading skills

### Materials

One copy of Blackline Master 50 per student; crayons

Explain to students that authors have different reasons for writing books. Some may want to teach a skill, some may want to persuade the reader to do something, and others may simply want to entertain their readers. Have students look over the illustrations and the sentences. If necessary, read aloud the sentences with students. Have them decide which student would probably like the story *Grass Sandals*. Invite students to color in that picture.

**INFORMAL ASSESSMENT**

To assess students' understanding of author's purpose, first turn to page 302 and read the text aloud. Ask what the author's purpose is here. (to teach about haiku and Japanese characters) Then read aloud the text on page 305, and ask what the author's purpose is here (to tell about Basho's life).

## Comprehension

**REVIEW MAKE JUDG-MENTS AND DECISIONS**
Blackline Master 51

### Objectives
- To develop understanding of making judgments and decisions
- To reinforce critical thinking
- To use illustrations

### Materials

One copy of Blackline Master 51 per student; pencils

Explain that people often make judgments and decisions by seeing what their choices are and choosing the one that they think will be the best. Have students look over the pictures and write whether or not they think Basho will enjoy each spot as a place to sleep. Ask them to explain their reasoning. Invite students to write about which bed they would choose to sleep in and why. If necessary, pair students needing language support with more advanced writers.

Read aloud the text on page 306. Ask students what judgment Basho makes and what he decides to do about it. (He is too restless to stay at home; he will walk across Japan.) Then ask students what judgment Basho makes about his hat and what he does about it. (It will blow away in the wind; he stitches a string onto his hat.)

## Vocabulary Strategy

**INTRODUCE CONTEXT CLUES**
Blackline Master 52

### Objectives
• To practice using context clues to define unfamiliar words
• To increase vocabulary
• To practice reading skills

### Materials

One copy of Blackline Master 52 per student; pencils

Remind students that the meaning of an unfamiliar word can often be found using surrounding words and pictures as clues. Then help them read the passage with the unfamiliar words printed in boldface. Encourage students to find the meaning of the boldfaced words using the context clues and picture clues. Finally, have them write each new word under the picture that best describes it.

**INFORMAL ASSESSMENT**

To assess students' ability to use context clues, turn to page 316 and point out the word *trotted*. Have students come up with a definition for the word by using the text and the illustration. Repeat the exercise on page 320 with the word *iris*.

# Author's Purpose

**Clues**

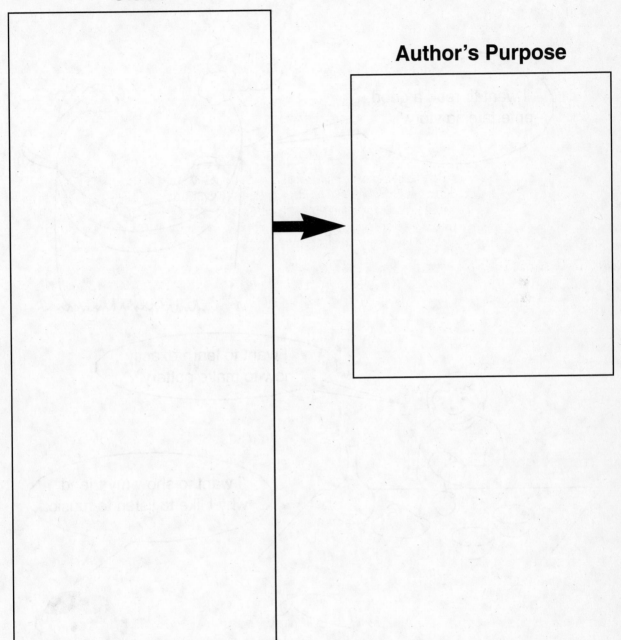

**Author's Purpose**

# Why Read It?

**1.** Color the person below who should read "Grass Sandals".

# Bedtime for Basho

1. Basho is tired and ready for bed. 2. Look at each bed shown below.
3. Tell why Basho does or does not like each bed. 4. Which bed would you choose to sleep in?

# Find the Picture

**1.** Read each word in dark print in the text below. **2.** Write the word in dark print on the line next to the picture it describes.

This is the story of a Haiku poet named Basho. He walked all over his country writing poetry. A friend once gave him a banana tree or **basho** which he planted near his **bamboo hut**. He liked the tree so much he decided to call himself Basho. Every morning he would have tea in his hut and look at the sea, mountains, and the **morning glories** right outside his door.

_____

_____

_____

# A PLACE CALLED FREEDOM pp. 332A–359P

Written by Scott Russell Sanders   Illustrated by Thomas B. Allen

## BUILD BACKGROUND FOR LANGUAGE SUPPORT

## I. FOCUS ON READING
### Focus on Skills

**OBJECTIVE:** Distinguish between fact and opinion

**TPR**

### Develop Visual Literacy

Have students look at the painting *The Migration of the Negro*, by Jacob Lawrence. Remind students that migration means moving from one place to another. Also explain that the people in the painting are moving from their old homes in the South to the big cities listed at the gates. Point to a color in the painting and say: *This is red. Is this true?* Point to another color and say *This is blue. Is this true.* Explain that these statements are true, and they are facts. Have students point to things they see in the painting that they can prove are true. (Possible answers: there are many people; they are walking through gates; some men are wearing hats.) Write students' answers on the left side of the chalkboard and label them *Facts*. Then say *Blue is the best color.* Explain to students that this is an opinion, a statement which cannot be proven. Then set up three "gates" in the classroom and label them Chicago, New York, and St. Louis. Have students choose a gate to line up in front of. Invite them to pretend they are the people in the painting, moving from their homes to a new city. Ask them to show and talk about which city they choose and why. Write answers on the right side of the board, explaining that these are opinions. Ask, *Do you like this painting? Why or why not?* Invite them to share and discuss their opinions about the painting.

## II. READ THE LITERATURE

### Vocabulary

**VOCABULARY**
plantation
settlement
fretted
gourd
sunrise
weary

Write the vocabulary words on the chalkboard. Say the words and have students repeat them after you. Ask three students to play the part of a mother, father, and child on a journey to a new place. Tell them to act out the scenes from the Teaching Chart as you read it aloud. Have the rest of the class guess the vocabulary word that is missing. Use as many context clues as necessary to help students choose the correct word. Or, you may read through the passage and skip a sentence as necessary. After you read each sentence, write the context clues on the chalkboard.

*The family lived and worked on the large _____ (plantation) for many years. One night, they left their home and started walking toward a small _____ (settlement) in Indiana. They heard that there were some nice people who lived in this community. The mother _____ (fretted) and worried that they were walking in the wrong direction. The father pointed to some stars in the shape of a big dipper. He called it "the drinking _____" (gourd) because it looked like a large, deep spoon used to hold water. Now, they knew they were going the right way. As a new day began, the family stopped and watched the beautiful _____ (sunrise). They were all tired and _____ (weary) from the long trip.*

Students can take turns playing the parts and acting out the scene.

**CONCEPT**

freedom

## Evaluate Prior Knowledge

To demonstrate the concept of freedom, show photographs of animals that are confined either in zoos or cages or kennels. Then show the same kinds of animals in free environments. For example, show a giraffe in a zoo, then show a giraffe running freely on the plains of Africa. Point to the cages around the animals and ask students what is different about the animals in each picture. Then have one volunteer walk to the front of the class and "cage" him or her, using chairs or desks. Show the rest of the class that the student can not move about freely. Then "release" the students and tell the class that he/she has gained his/her freedom. Explain that some people have also lived without freedom, struggled for it, and finally gained it. Invite students to share what they know about slavery and what it means to be free.

**TPR**

## Develop Oral Language

Use pictures of caged animals, or bring in other pictures illustrating African American history and plantation life. Ask students to study the pictures and to think what it feels like not to have freedom. Invite students to pantomime examples of what it means to have freedom, such as being an animal in the wilderness, being a person who once did not have choices but who now does, and so on. Give students the option to work alone or in small groups.

nonverbal prompt for active participation

one- or two-word response prompt

prompt for short answers to higher-level thinking skills

prompt for detailed answers to higher-level thinking skills

• Preproduction: *Show us* (point to class and self) *what it is like not to have freedom. Now show us* (point to class and self) *what it is like to gain and have freedom.*

• Early production: *Are you sad when you are not free? Are you happy when you are free?*

• Speech emergence: *Tell us the name of the animal or person you are acting out that has freedom. Where does* (name of animal or person) *live when it's free? Where does* (name of animal or person) *live when it's not free?*

• Intermediate fluency: *How does it feel when you are not free? Why do you think freedom is important?*

# Guided Instruction

## Preview and Predict

Tell students that this is a story about an African American family in the early 1800s who are freed from slavery and move north to settle as free people. Turn to the title page and ask a volunteer to read the title aloud. Give students time to look over the illustration, and then ask: *Who do you think the people in the picture are? What are they doing?* After listening to students' predictions, guide them through the selection to preview the story and make predictions. Along the way, ask questions such as: *Where is the family going? Who do you think the man with the boat is? Why might he be important to the family? How does the family spend their time together? Who are the other people that show up? Why do you think they appear? What kind of work do the family and their friends do? Why is there a sign that says Freedom at the train station? What do you think the boy is writing at the end of the story?*

**GRAPHIC ORGANIZER**

Blackline Master 53

## Objectives

• To distinguish between fact and opinion
• To practice writing skills
• To develop critical thinking

## Materials

One copy of Blackline Master 53 per student; pencils

Remind students that a fact is a piece of information that can be proved true or false, while an opinion is a thought or belief someone has about something. Explain to students that we can learn about characters in a story from the opinions they express. Ask students to pause while reading the story to fill in the chart with facts and opinions they have learned. Explain to students that some opinions in stories may be expressed by the narrator, or other characters in the story. For example, after reading the first paragraph on p. 340, ask: *Is it a fact or opinion that the fisherman has a face as wrinkled as an old boot?* (opinion) *Why? The narrator feels that the old man's face is so wrinkled, it is his opinion.* You may want to pair native English speakers with those needing additional language support to work together filling out the chart.

# III. BUILD SKILLS

## Comprehension

### REVIEW FACT AND OPINION
Blackline Master 54

### Objectives
• To distinguish between fact and opinion
• To use critical thinking
• To use illustrations

### Materials

One copy of Blackline Master 54 per student; pencils

Review the definitions of fact and opinion with students. A fact is a statement that can be proven. An opinion is a statement of what someone thinks or feels. Then explain that in each picture one character states a fact while the other states an opinion. Have students review the pictures and read the statements. Ask students to decide which statement is a fact and which one is an opinion, and write fact or opinion on the appropriate line under each picture. To help students, point out that they can look for clue words and phrases such as *I think*, *I feel*, etc. which show opinions.

### INFORMAL ASSESSMENT

To assess students' ability to distinguish between fact and opinion, read aloud the top paragraph on page 343 and ask students to state a fact and an opinion about the family's first year. (Opinion- Papa could grow anything; Fact – Papa raised crops to buy land; he could handle horses; he could build a barn or a bed.)

## Comprehension

### REVIEW SUMMARIZE
Blackline Master 55

### Objectives
• To review skills used in summarizing
• To recall story details

### Materials

One copy of Blackline Master 55 per pair of students

Tell students that a person can summarize a story by retelling the most important parts of the story in their own words. Review the pictures on the worksheet with students. Explain that with a partner students will pretend to be the character in the story and summarize the story by using the pictures on the page. Have partners take turns pointing to each picture and telling what is happening. Invite partners to use the pictures to summarize the story *A Place Called Freedom* in their own words.

**INFORMAL ASSESSMENT**    To assess students' ability to summarize, turn to the illustration on page 338 and ask them to tell in their own words the most important information about this scene. (The family is traveling at night to reach the North where they can be free.) Repeat the exercise on page 344 where more people arrive from the South.

## Vocabulary Strategy

**REVIEW CONTEXT CLUES**
Blackline Master 56

### Objectives

• To identify context clues to understand the meanings of unfamiliar words
• To increase vocabulary
• To practice critical thinking

### Materials

One copy of Blackline Master 56 per student; crayons

Explain to students that the meaning of unfamiliar words can sometimes be found in the context, or words around them. Pictures which accompany the text can also provide clues to unfamiliar words. Have students read each unfamiliar word in the left column and then the clue word in the middle column. Ask students to circle the picture that best describes each word.

**INFORMAL ASSESSMENT**    To assess students' skill at using context clues, turn to page 347 and point out the word *barrel*. Then invite students to read through the surrounding words and to look at the illustration in order to understand the word's meaning. Repeat the exercise on page 339 with the word *glittery*.

# Fact and Opinion

| Fact | Opinion |
|------|---------|
|      |         |

# Fact or Opinion?

**1.** Write "Fact" under each fact, something that is true. **2.** Write "Opinion" next to each opinion, something that someone thinks or believes.

# Photos for the Album

**1.** The boy on the left is showing us pictures of how Freedom became a town.
**2.** Describe what happens in each picture.

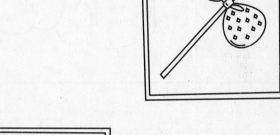

# Find the Meaning

1. Read each word. 2. Read each clue to understand its meaning. 3. Circle the picture that goes with the word.

| Word | Clue | Meaning |
|------|------|---------|
| gourd | | |
| plantation | | |
| sunrise | | |

# TWISTED TRAILS pp. 360A–369P

## BUILD BACKGROUND FOR LANGUAGE SUPPORT

## I. FOCUS ON READING
### Focus on Skills

- - - - - - - - - - - - - - - - - - - - - - - - - - - - - - - - - - - - - - -

### Develop Visual Literacy

**OBJECTIVE:** Make judgments and decisions

**TPR**

Invite students to look at the picture *Relativity,* by M.C. Escher. Ask them to try to judge first where the floors are and then where the walls are. Challenge their decisions by having them touch each wall and floor. Invite volunteers to point out to the class where they think the walls and the floors are. Lead them to see that most walls in the picture are also floors and vice versa. Challenge them to find floors that serve as walls and to explain how they reached the decision. Ask students: *Why do you think the artist decided to create a picture like this? Will the people in the picture ever get to where they are going? Why not?* Invite students to pretend they are a person in the picture. Ask, *Where would you be?* After listening to students' answers, invite them to draw their own picture or create a three dimensional structure that challenges viewer's initial judgments, as this etching does. Have students share their completed drawings with the class.

## II. READ THE LITERATURE

### Vocabulary

**VOCABULARY**
challenge
entertaining
mazes
combine
requires
contained

Write the vocabulary words on the chalkboard. Then, on a large table, create two separate mazes with wooden blocks or other items from the classroom. Have students gather around as you demonstrate the meaning of each vocabulary word. With a doll or toy "walk" through the mazes. Say: *Here are two mazes. They have paths that are contained inside walls. I will combine them to make one big maze. Now the challenge is for* (name doll or toy) *to get from one end to the other. It is hard, but it is also entertaining.* (name of doll or toy) *has fun. The maze requires* (name of doll or toy) *to think about how to get to the other end!*

Go through the whole story once, then repeat it, stopping at each vocabulary word and having students define it. Continue working with that word until the class comes to a consensus about its correct meaning.

Then organize students into small groups. Give each group a set of 15 to 20 blocks. Invite them to build a maze and write sentences about their maze using the vocabulary words. Have groups trade mazes, with one student doing a finger walk through the maze while another student reads the sentences aloud.

### Evaluate Prior Knowledge

**CONCEPT**
careers

Bring in items used by people in certain professions, and act out the tasks of each person. For example, with a pouch and envelope, demonstrate being a postal carrier; with a hammer and nail, act out being a carpenter; with a stethoscope and a thermometer, pretend to be a doctor. As students watch and listen, ask them what you are doing and what all the demonstrations have in common. Repeat the exercises until students conclude that you are demonstrating the careers that some people have.

## Develop Oral Language

Invite students to demonstrate using body language or pantomime a career with which they are familiar. They may wish to work individually, with partners, or in small groups to create situations such as those modeled by you.

- Preproduction: *Show us* (point to class and self) *the career you have chosen.*

- Early production: *Do you know someone who is a* (name of career title)*? Would you like to be a* (name of career title) *some day?*

- Speech emergence: *What is your career called? Where is this kind of work done?*

- Intermediate fluency: *How would you feel about being a* (name of career title)*? Why would you like it? Why might it be hard or easy?*

# Guided Instruction

### Preview and Predict

Tell students that this selection is about a man named Adrian Fisher, who makes giant mazes as a career. Invite students to predict how Mr. Fisher makes his mazes. Write their predictions on the board. Then show students the first two pages of the selection. Ask: *Why do you think these mazes are all outside?* Allow students time to answer your question, and then ask: *Where else might mazes be built?* After students make their predictions, turn to the next page and show them the maze that is placed in the middle of a pool at the Getty Museum. Next, ask students what people they think might be best at making their way through mazes. Ask them how they would work their way through a maze like one made by Adrian Fisher.

### Objectives

- To understand judgment and decision making
- To use illustrations

### Materials

One copy of Blackline Master 57 per student; pencils

Help students use the two-column chart to create a list of the judgments and decisions made in this selection. Invite them to write about the judgments and decisions of the maze maker or of the people walking through the mazes.

To further reinforce judgments, have students work in pairs. Have one partner pretend to be a reporter, while the other pretends to be the maze maker. The reporter can ask the maze maker questions about why she or he decided to make certain kinds of mazes. These decisions can be reported on the chart.

# III. BUILD SKILLS

## Comprehension

**REVIEW AUTHOR'S PURPOSE AND POINT OF VIEW**
Blackline Master 58

**Objectives**
- To understand author's purpose
- To practice critical thinking
- To practice writing skills

**Materials**

One copy of Blackline Master 58 per student; pencils

Remind students that people have different reasons for doing things. Some people do things in order to teach, others do things to entertain, and so on. Explain that different points of view also make people do things for different reasons. Then have students write in the appropriate space what purpose they think people might have for building mazes. Encourage them to use a group of words from the top of the page in their answers.

**INFORMAL ASSESSMENT**

To assess students' understanding of author's purpose and point of view, have them review the selection and talk about what the purpose was in writing the story. (to tell about the work of a certain maze maker) Then ask them to pretend to be farmers growing corn. *What could their purpose be? How might their point of view about the maze maker change?*

## Vocabulary Strategy

**REVIEW CONTEXT CLUES**
Blackline Master 59

**Objectives**
- To organize information
- To increase vocabulary

**Materials**

One copy of Blackline Master 59 per student; pencils

Invite students to follow the path from start to finish. As they go along, tell them to write the letter they find at each dead end. When they have finished the maze, have them unscramble the letters to find the new word.

**INFORMAL ASSESSMENT**

To assess students' ability to use context clues, turn their attention to page 364. Help them read the first paragraph and invite volunteers to define the word *roadblock*. Remind them that other words in the sentence will help them find the word's meaning. Repeat the exercise on the following page with the word *professional*.

# Vocabulary Strategy

**INFORMAL ASSESSMENT**

## Objectives

• To develop understanding of suffixes
• To increase vocabulary
• To use critical thinking

## Materials

One copy of Blackline Master 60 per student; scissors; paste or glue; pencils

Invite students to follow the maze from the words to the suffixes at the end. Ask students to choose the suffix at the end of each maze that creates a new word when added to the word on the left. Have students write the three new words on the lines provided. Invite them to say the new words aloud. Invite volunteers to explain each word's meaning.

To assess students' recognition of suffixes, turn to the first sentence of the second paragraph on page 363. Ask students to find and break down the word containing a suffix. *(careful: care + -ful)* Repeat the exercise on the following page with the paragraph containing the word *colorful*.

# Judgments and Decisions

**Judgments**

**Decision**

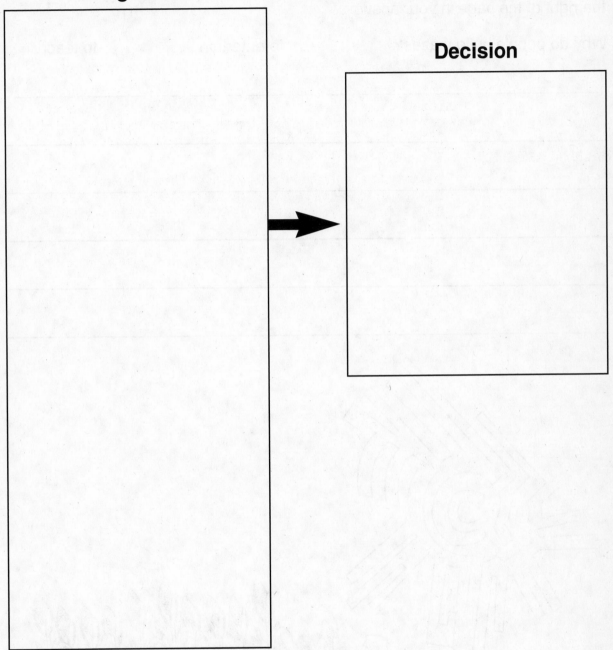

# How You Look At It

**1.** Write a sentence to answer the question. **2.** Use one of the words shown on the right of the page in your answer.

Why do people build mazes?          to entertain          to teach

_____

_____

_____

_____

_____

_____

# Be Amazed!

**1.** Follow the path from Start to Finish. **2.** Collect the letters at each dead-end, where you have to back up. **3.** Write each dead-end letter in a box.
**4.** Unscramble the letters to make a word. **5.** Write the word at the finish line.

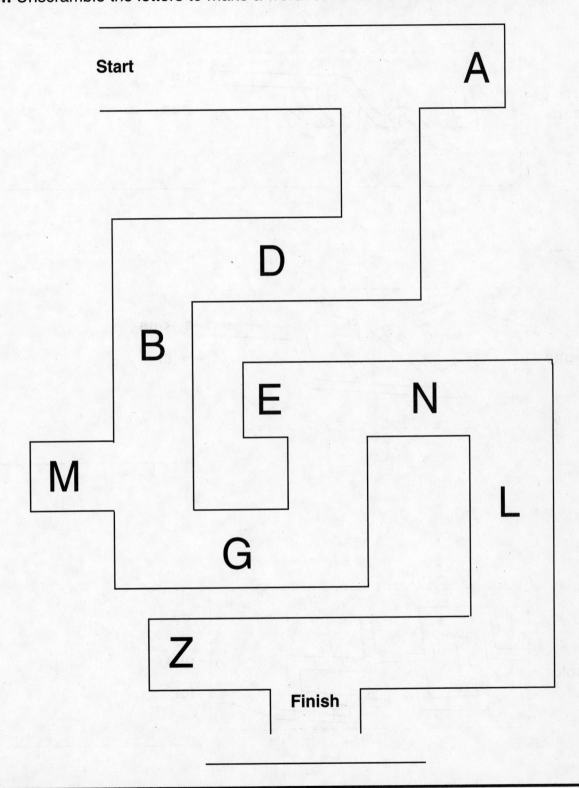

# Maze Mania

**1.** Read each word at the beginning of each maze. **2.** Follow the maze. **3.** Write the correct word you find at the end.

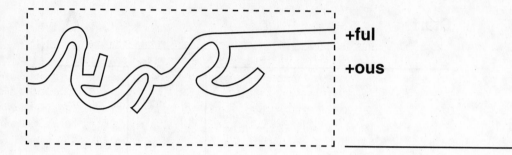

**1. care**    +ful

+ous

_____

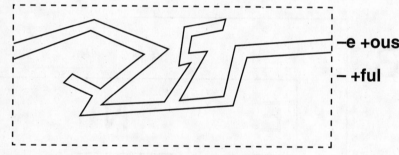

**2. fame**    –e +ous

– +ful

_____

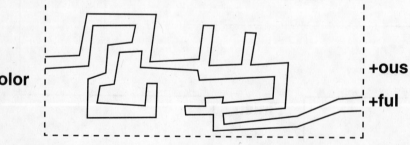

**3. color**    +ous

+ful

_____

# SCRUFFY pp. 374A–405P

Written by Jim Brandenburg  Photographs by Jim Brandenburg

## BUILD BACKGROUND FOR LANGUAGE SUPPORT

# I. FOCUS ON READING

## Focus on Skills

**OBJECTIVE:** Compare and contrast

**TPR**

### Develop Visual Literacy

Direct students' attention to the picture of the dog in the garden. Ask students to point to different things they see in the painting. Guide them to see flowers, the dog, a spider, a butterfly, a frog. Now, point to a pansy and say *flower*. Say: *Point to a flower that is the same as this. Point to a flower that is different.* Repeat with other objects in the painting. Have children point to items with similarities or differences by giving prompts such as: *This flower is (name of color). Point to something else that is the same color. What size is the dog? Point to an animal that is a different size than the dog.* Encourage more proficient students to explain why two things are the same or different.

# II. READ THE LITERATURE

### Vocabulary

**VOCABULARY**
climate
methods
injury
clinging
threat
affection

Write the vocabulary words on cards and hold up each word as you use it in a simple sentence. Use repetition, facial expressions, and body language to help students understand word meaning. For example: *A bigger wolf can be a threat to a pup. The climate of the North Pole is very cold. A wolf's bite can cause injury. The wolf shows affection by licking and caressing. The pups are clinging to their mother. Scruffy uses different methods, or ways, to train the pups.* Then say each sentence from Teaching Chart 92, leaving out the vocabulary words. Have volunteers point to the vocabulary word which completes each sentence.

### Evaluate Prior Knowledge

**CONCEPT**
photography

Show students some photographs and drawings or paintings of similar subjects. Explain that photographers use a camera to capture images, while artists may use pencils or paints. Have them identify which medium makes the subject look more real. Take students to the library, or bring in a variety of things for students to look at which contain photographs, such as books, magazines, newspapers, yearbooks, or photo albums. Discuss the photographs you find, and the different reasons people have for taking them. Ask students why they think the author used photographs for this story about Arctic wolves.

### Develop Oral Language

Bring in a camera for students to use. (A Polaroid camera would be especially fun.) Invite students to take photographs of things in or around the school which interest them. Use prompts appropriate for the linguistic level of students.

**nonverbal prompt for active participation**

• Preproduction: *Take a picture* (point to student, then model taking a picture with the camera) *of something or someone* (indicate the class, and classroom)

**one- or two-word response prompt**

• Early production: *What did you take a picture of? Where will you put your picture?*

**prompt for short answers to higher-level thinking skills**

• Speech emergence: *What did you take a picture of? Why did you want to take that picture? What will you do with your photograph?*

**prompt for detailed answers to higher-level thinking skills**

• Intermediate fluency: *Tell us about your picture and why you took it. What other pictures would you like to take? Why? Have you taken any other pictures? Tell us about them.*

## Guided Instruction

### Preview and Predict

Read the title and the author's name. Explain that Jim Brandenburg took the photographs first, and then wrote the story. Use the photographs to generate discussion of photography, and encourage students to make predictions about the story. Ask questions such as: *What do you think this story will be about? Do you think the story is about real wolves or made up animals? What makes you think this? What do you think you might learn by reading this story? How do you think the photographs might help you learn this? Would you want to read this story if it had illustrations instead of photographs? Why or why not?* Then have students write questions they hope will be answered in the story. If necessary, pair a fluent English speaker with a student needing language support, and have the fluent student act as a recorder. Post students' questions, and return to them after reading the story to see whether they were answered.

**GRAPHIC ORGANIZER**
Blackline Master 61

### Objectives

• To practice comparing and contrasting
• To reinforce understanding of character details
• To encourage higher-level thinking skills

### Materials

One copy of Blackline Master 61 per two students; pencils

Organize students into pairs. As you read the story, stop and discuss the similarities and differences students find between Scruffy and the other wolves. For example, after reading page 384 ask students: *How is Scruffy different from the more dominant wolves? What is different about the way he looks and moves? What is different about how he gets food?* Have students discuss with their partners the differences they find, and record them on their chart. After reading page 393, help students identify similarities between Scruffy and the alpha male by asking questions such as: *How is Scruffy's job like the alpha male's job?* Ask questions to help students contrast Scruffy's behavior when he is alone with the pups to the times he is with the rest of the pack. For example: *How does Scruffy move when he is with the pups? How does he move when the other wolves are around? What is different about the way Scruffy acts with the pups, than how he acts with the other wolves?* Call on pairs to share the similarities and differences they find.

# III. BUILD SKILLS

## Comprehension

**COMPARE AND CONTRAST**
Blackline Master 62

**Objectives**
- To make comparisons and contrast based on a story
- To support hands-on learning

**Materials**

One copy of Blackline Master 62 per student; colored pencils or crayons; pencils

Explain to students that stories often compare and contrast characters to show how they are alike or different. Tell students that in each picture, the two wolves are different in some way. Have students look at each pair of wolves, and decide what is different. Invite them to color the things that are different in each pair of wolves, and write what is different on the line.

**INFORMAL ASSESSMENT**

Display a picture of a dog and a cat for students. Then ask students to write three statements comparing and contrasting these animals.

## Comprehension

**DRAW CONCLUSIONS**
Blackline Master 63

**Objectives**
- To draw a conclusion based on logic
- To encourage higher-level thinking skills
- To support cooperative learning

**Materials**

One copy of Blackline Master 63 per two students; pencils

Explain to students that the author of Scruffy watched the wolves in order to learn about them. He gathered information in order to draw conclusions about the wolves. Go over the page with students. Discuss the pictures and help students read the text on the right side. Have students work together to match a picture on the left side of the page with the conclusion the author drew. Have them draw a line from each picture to its conclusion.

**INFORMAL ASSESSMENT**

Ask students to turn to page 384. Read the second paragraph together. Have students identify the conclusion the author drew about Scruffy. (Scruffy was the lowest-ranking member of the pack.) Encourage them to identify the facts that support this conclusion. (He ate last and had to beg for food; he was beaten.)

**INTRODUCE PREFIXES**
Blackline Master 64

### Objectives

- To identify prefixes and determine meaning
- To reinforce vocabulary development
- To practice following directions

### Materials

One copy of Blackline Master 64 per student; pencils

Tell students that adding a prefix to a word can change its meaning. Have students read the words in the left column. Help them identify any unfamiliar words. Then tell them to add the prefix *dis-* to each word in the right column to create a new word that matches the picture. Have students read the new words aloud. If necessary, model adding *dis-* to the first word. Ask students to guess what the prefix *dis-* means. (opposite of)

**INFORMAL ASSESSMENT**

Tell students to turn to page 399. Have them identify the word with the prefix *dis-*, and tell what it means. (disappeared) Ask them to remove the prefix, and read the resulting word. Discuss its meaning and invite students to use the word in a sentence. Then write the following words on the board: *agree, continue, grace.* Have students form new words by adding *dis-* to each word. Ask students to use each new word in a sentence.

# Compare and Contrast

| Similarities | Differences |
|---|---|
|  |  |

# Alike and Different

**1.** Color in how the wolves are different. **2.** Write what is different on the line.

_____    _____

_____    _____

# Figuring It Out

1. On the left side of the page are scenes the author saw on his trip. 2. On the right side of the page are some of the conclusions he made. 3. Draw a line from the scene to the correct conclusion the author made.

# Change the Meaning

**1.** Write *dis-* in each blank to make a new word. **2.** In the space above the new word draw a picture of each new word.

**appear**

_____

**approve**

_____

**obey**

_____

**cover**

_____

# GLUSKABE AND THE SNOW BIRD pp. 406A–423P

Written by Joseph Bruchac  Illustrated by Stefano Vitale

## BUILD BACKGROUND FOR LANGUAGE SUPPORT

# I. FOCUS ON READING

## Focus on Skills

### Develop Visual Literacy

**OBJECTIVE:** Distinguish between fact and nonfact

**TPR**

Give students a physical symbol for True (hold one finger up)  and for False (hold two fingers up). Ask students True/False questions. *I am five years old. I am wearing a hat. I am wearing yellow. We are in the park.* Then have a volunteer ask True/False questions with the class responding with the physical prompt. Now, ask students True/False questions related to the picture. Look at the picture with students. Have them touch the sun and name it. Ask: *Is there really a sun in the sky? Does the real sun look like this one? Point to and touch the parts of the sun that do not look real.* Then have students point to the stars in the picture. Ask: *Are there really stars in the sky? Do real stars look like these? How are these stars like real stars? How are they different?* Encourage students to identify other things in the picture that are not as they appear in real life.

Invite students to draw their own scenes that include facts and nonfacts.

# II. READ THE LITERATURE

### Vocabulary

**VOCABULARY**
confusion
lodge
messenger
hilltop
freeze
praised

Write the vocabulary words on the chalkboard and have students copy the words onto a piece of paper. Using body language and facial expressions, read the following sentence from the story stressing vocabulary words as pronounced. *The people praised Gluskabe for doing great things. They slept and ate in Gluskabe's lodge. One day a messenger came from the north. A big bird stood above them on the hilltop. Cover the plants so they do not freeze when it snows. When the sun did not shine, there was confusion and no one knew what to do.* Divide the class into six groups and assign each group one of the vocabulary words.  Using the materials in the classroom have each group reach a consensus as to the definition of each word.  Have each group member make a simple drawing which will define the word.  You might suggest the following, for *freeze* draw a person bundled up with teeth chattering. For *praised* draw an audience applauding a man on stage. *Messenger:* draw a person carrying a bag full of mail. *Lodge:* draw a log cabin. *Confusion:* draw a woman in the middle of a crowd looking lost. *Hilltop:* profile of a hill with arrow pointing to top.  Have students take turns presenting their pictures as the class guesses which word the picture defines.

### Evaluate Prior Knowledge

**CONCEPT**
myths

Show the class pictures depicting the seasons and atmospheric changes of each. For example, a picture of a rainy spring day, a picture of a snow covered street. Ask them what each depicts, and where it comes from. As students tell what they know about rain and snow, draw a simple water cycle on the board to illustrate the process. Then tell students that long ago people tried to explain where rain, snow and other things in nature came from, and they had many different ideas. These explanations were often not based on facts, and were told in stories called myths.

### Develop Oral Language

nonverbal prompt for active participation

- Preproduction: *Show us* (point to self and class) *how you* (point to student) *could make* (name type of weather and point to a picture of it) *if you* (point to student) *were as tall as the sky.* (point to the sky)

one- or two-word response prompt

- Early production: *Where does* (name type of weather) *come from in your myth? What other things look and feel like* (name type of weather)*? Do they come in the same way?*

prompt for short answers to higher-level thinking skills

- Speech emergence: *Tell us about your myth. Who creates* (name type of weather)*? How?*

prompt for detailed answers to higher-level thinking skills

- Intermediate fluency: *What can you compare to* (name type of weather)*? How are they alike? How can that help you explain where* (name type of weather) *comes from? Tell about a person or animal in a myth that could make (*name type of weather)*. How would she or he make it? Why would she or he make* name type of weather)*?*

## Guided Instruction

### Preview and Predict

Tell students that this story is a myth that explains several things in nature. Read the title together, and have students identify Gluskabe and the Snow Bird in the illustrations on the title page. Explain that Gluskabe is a giant, a person much taller than ordinary people. As you lead students through the story, have them identify illustration details that seem to be from real life, and those that are make-believe. Encourage students to make predictions and think about parts of the story that might be fact and parts that might be nonfact. Ask questions such as: *Do you think Gluskabe is real? Show us something in a picture that makes you think this. How is the skunk like a real skunk? How is it different? What do you think Gluskabe is saying to the Snow Bird? Do you think the Snow Bird and the Day Eagle are real birds? Point to something in a picture that makes you think this. What seems to happen to Skunk? Why do you think this happens?* Have students discuss with a partner what natural things might be explained in the story. For example, why Skunk's color changes, why it stops snowing, and what makes day and night. Students should record their ideas and share them with the class.

**GRAPHIC ORGANIZER**
Blackline Master 65

### Objectives

- To practice drawing conclusions
- To practice distinguishing fact from nonfact

### Materials

One copy of Blackline Master 65 per student; pencils

Go over the chart with students, making sure to explain that the *Fact* column is for recording things that can be proved or are based on facts, and the *Nonfact* column is where they will record things that cannot be proved or are based on nonfacts. As you read the story, stop periodically and discuss what is a fact and what is a nonfact. For example, after reading pages 414–415, ask students what facts they read about snow. (It covers plants. When it melts, it fills rivers and lakes. It snows for only part of the year.) Help them record these things in the *Fact* column on their charts. Students needing additional language support can copy phrases from the board or draw small pictures. Then repeat the activity with things they read about snow that are nonfact. (Snow Bird makes it snow). Continue the activity with facts and nonfacts from other pages.

# III. BUILD SKILLS

## Comprehension

**FACT AND NONFACT**
Blackline Master 66

### Objectives
• To practice distinguishing fact from nonfact
• To encourage deductive thinking skills

### Materials
One copy of Blackline 66 per student; scissors; paste or glue

Go over the page with students, helping them read any unfamiliar words. Point out that the books on the bookshelves on the left are about real things that could be proved. The books on the bookshelves on the right are about unreal things that could not be proved. Have students cut out the books at the bottom, and paste each one on the correct shelf, depending on whether the book being cut out is based on fact or nonfact.

**INFORMAL ASSESSMENT**

Have students work with a partner. Assign a page from the story to each pair, and tell them to find something on the page that is a fact and something that is a nonfact. Call on teams to share what they find.

## Comprehension

**COMPARE AND CONTRAST**
Blackline Master 67

### Objectives
• To practice finding similarities and differences
• To encourage the use of visual clues

### Materials
One copy of Blackline Master 67 per student; pencils

Have students identify what is happening in each picture. Then tell them to compare each pair of pictures and determine how they are alike and how they are different. Guide students to write words or phrases that describe the similarities and differences on the correct lines under each pair of pictures.

**INFORMAL ASSESSMENT**

Direct students to pages 414–415 and 416–417. Have pairs of students compare and contrast the Snow Bird and the Day Eagle. Invite them to share the similarities and differences they found between the two birds.

## ROOT WORDS
Blackline Master 68

### Objectives
• To practice finding root words
• To develop vocabulary

### Materials

One copy of Blackline Master 68 per student; pencils

Tell students that prefixes are added in front of a root word and suffixes to the end of a root word to form new words. Encourage students to read the word problem under each picture. Explain how to subtract a suffix to find a root word. Tell students to then solve each problem and write the root word on the line under the picture. Encourage students to read the root words they have written to a partner.

## INFORMAL ASSESSMENT

Direct students to turn to page 416. Read the first sentence together. Then ask students to identify the root words in *melting* and *walked*. Challenge them to find as many other words with suffixes as they can, and then identify their root words.

# Fact and Nonfact

| Fact | Nonfact |
|------|---------|
|      |         |

# Real or Not?

**1.** Cut out the books at the bottom of the page. **2.** Paste the books where they belong.

| **Books About Real Things** | **Books About Make-Believe Things** |
|---|---|

Have Fun
With Food

The Life
of
Dr. Martin
Luther King

Pigs with
Wings

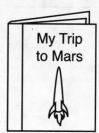
My Trip
to Mars

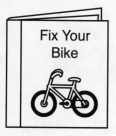
Fix Your
Bike

Fairy
Tales

Charlie
Bear

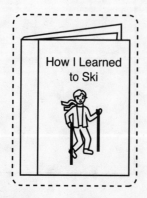
How I Learned
to Ski

The
Barge
Monster

Fish
Science

# Find the Differences

1. Look at each pair of pictures. 2. Write the name of what is different. 3. Write the name of what is the same.

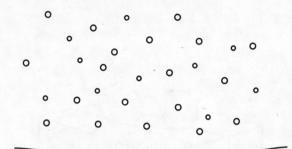

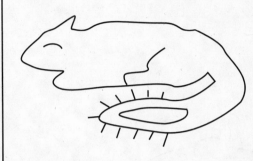

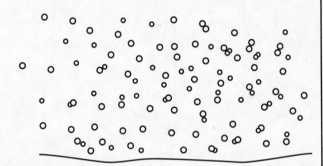

Alike _____    Alike _____

Different _____    Different _____

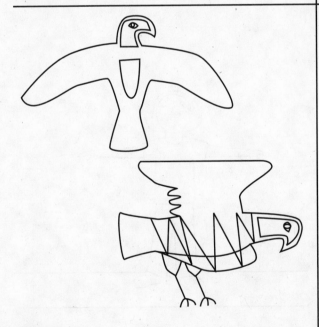

Alike _____    Alike _____

Different _____    Different _____

# Word Arithmetic

**1.** Write the new words.

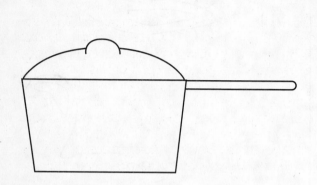

cooked – ed = _____    tightly – ly = _____

falling – ing = _____    careful – ful = _____

Written and Illustrated by Luise Woelflein and photographed by David Doubilet

## BUILD BACKGROUND FOR LANGUAGE SUPPORT

## I. FOCUS ON READING
### Focus on Skills

**OBJECTIVE:** Draw conclusions

**TPR**

### Develop Visual Literacy

Read the title of the painting *Broken Pieces of Colored Glassware* by Jonathan Blair to the class. Ask students to draw a picture of what they think the painting might look like based on the title. Then as you look at the picture together, ask students what they see. Tell them to point to the piece of glass with the star shape. Ask: *What shape do you see? Does this piece of glass look new or old? Touch another piece that looks old. What makes it look old?* Have students point to the blue bottle in the upper right. Ask: *Does this look rough or smooth? Touch something that is smooth. What do you think made the glass smooth? Where do you think this bottle was found?* Remind students that stories (and pictures) don't always tell us everything. Help them draw conclusions about why the artist might have painted this picture. Then invite students to choose one piece of glass from the picture. Have them draw what they think the original jar or bottle looked like before it was broken. Encourage students to share their drawings with the class. Have them explain how they came to their conclusions.

## II. READ THE LITERATURE

**VOCABULARY**
endangered
sponge
poisonous
connected
haul
overcome

### Vocabulary

Invite the class to suppose what it must be like deep in the ocean where very few people have ever been. Tell students that there are many varieties of life in the oceans. Write the vocabulary words on the chalkboard. Say the words and have students repeat them after you. Tell the class that they are going to put on a small play and that several volunteers are needed to play the characters in the play. Explain to the class that they should try to think about what a sea creature might be thinking when it sees an underwater explorer for the first time. Also ask students: *What might the explorer be thinking?* Have one student play the part of an underwater explorer and several other students to play the part of sea creatures. Tell them to act out the following scene as you read it. Have the students who are watching guess the vocabulary word that is missing in the following sentences:

*The scientist was swimming deep in the ocean looking for sea creatures. Many of the animals were hard to find because of overfishing and pollution. These animals are _____ (endangered). The scientist did find a giant basket _____ (sponge). She swam inside the _____ (sponge) just to see what was inside. Suddenly, a _____ (poisonous) lionfish stung her on the arm. Luckily, she was _____ (connected) to the boat with a rope. She used the rope to _____ (haul) herself out of the water. This was another problem that she had to _____ (overcome).*

Students may take turns playing the parts and acting out the scene.

### Evaluate Prior Knowledge

Bring in photos of various types of marine life. Be sure to include plants and a variety of animals. (For example: jellyfish, dolphins, whales, sponges, seaweed, and clams.) Help students name the animals and plants in the photos. Invite them to guess what all the plants and animals have in common. (they all live in the ocean) Then ask students to sort the pictures into two groups: plants and animals. Some, like sponges or coral, can be confusing, and students will need additional information from you. Have students note similarities and differences among the animals, and again among the plants. If possible, show a video that lets students see marine creatures moving underwater.

### Develop Oral Language

Invite students to draw their favorite marine animal or plant. Ask students, one at a time, to show their pictures to the rest of the group. Use prompts appropriate for students' linguistic level.

nonverbal prompt for active participation

- Preproduction: *Stand up and show us your picture. Point to the* (name of creature). *Show us how you think it moves in the water. Point to another animal that is the same color/size.*

one- or two-word response prompt

- Early production: *Show us your picture. What is it? Is* (name of marine life) *a plant or an animal? What color is it? Is it big or little? What is it doing? What does it eat? Do other animals eat (name of marine life)?*

prompt for short answers to higher-level thinking skills

- Speech emergence: *Show us your picture. What is it? Describe the (*name of plant or animal). *What do you know about it? What is it doing? Why do you think it is doing that?*

prompt for detailed answers to higher-level thinking skills

- Intermediate fluency: *What picture do you have? Describe the (name of plant or animal). How is it like some of the other animals/plants in the pictures? How is it different? Why do you like it? Have you ever seen one? Tell us about it.*

## Guided Instruction

### Preview and Predict

Read the title and the author's name. Tell students this story is about Sylvia Earle, who is a marine biologist. Explain that a marine biologist is a scientist. Have students page through the photographs to figure out what a marine biologist does. Use the photographs to reinforce the concept of marine life and to encourage students to make predictions about the story. Ask questions such as: *What do we call the type of illustrations used in this story?* (photographs) *Do you think this story is fiction (made-up) or nonfiction (real)? What makes you think that? Point to a picture of something that lives in the sea. What do you think it is? Do you think it's a plant or an animal? Find a picture that shows special clothes or equipment that Sylvia uses. What do you think it is? How do you think it helps her?* Then ask students to generate questions they have about Sylvia and her work. Record these questions on a chart or the chalkboard. After reading the story, go over the questions to see which ones were answered and which ones require further research.

**GRAPHIC ORGANIZER**
Blackline Master 69

### Objectives
• To practice drawing conclusions
• To practice comparing and contrasting
• To reinforce understanding of story details

### Materials
One copy of Blackline Master 69 per two students; pencils

Go over the chart headings with students. As you read the story, stop periodically and help students draw conclusions from the text. In the left column, have them record story events that lead them to their conclusions. In the right column, have them compare or contrast these events with things they already know. For example, after reading page 427, ask students to talk about what kind of person Sylvia is. Then ask them to compare or contrast what they read about her with what they know from personal experience. On the left side of the chart they might write about Sylvia's encounters with dangerous animals. On the right side they might write that most people would stay away from such creatures. Point out that these two pieces of information might draw them to conclude that Sylvia is brave.

# III. BUILD SKILLS
## Comprehension

**REVIEW DRAW CONCLUSIONS**
Blackline Master 70

### Objectives
• To practice drawing conclusions
• To reinforce using picture clues
• To support higher-level thinking skills

### Materials
One copy of Blackline Master 70 per student; pencils

Review the page with students, making sure they can identify each picture. Have them look at the first picture in the left column. Ask them where they think the animals and plants live. Then have students draw a line from the animals to the pictures of their environments. When the page is completed, invite students to share what they know about the animals and environments. Encourage them to explain how they arrived at their answers.

**INFORMAL ASSESSMENT**

Direct students to the text on page 433 and the picture on page 435. Ask them to describe what they think the Jim Suit is like (thick/thin, light/heavy, stiff/flexible) based on what they have read about divers and water pressure.

# Comprehension

**REVIEW FACT AND NONFACT**
Blackline Master 71

**Objectives**
• To practice distinguishing fact from nonfact
• To encourage higher-level thinking skills
• To support hands-on learning

**Materials**

One copy of Blackline Master 71 per student; crayons

Have students look carefully at each fish and color only the fish that could not be real. Invite students to share their reasons for deciding which fish are real and which are not.

**INFORMAL ASSESSMENT**

Direct students back to *Meet an Underwater Explorer.* Have students find information in the text or illustrations to support their opinions.

# Vocabulary Strategy

**ROOT WORDS**
Blackline Master 72

**Objectives**
• To practice identifying root words
• To support structural analysis
• To practice following directions

**Materials**

One copy of Blackline Master 72 per student; pencils

Have students read the word in the first picture. Tell them to remove the suffix *-ist* and add the suffix *-y*, as indicated in the "equation." Have students write the root word on the line. Make sure they can read the original words and understand which prefix/suffix to drop. Have students share their answers with a partner.

**INFORMAL ASSESSMENT**

Have students work in small groups. Assign each team a page of text, and challenge them to find as many words with suffixes or prefixes as they can. Have them list the original word with the root word next to it. Call on teams to share their words.

# Draw Conclusions

| What I Read | What I Know |
|---|---|
| | |

# Where Are You?

**1.** Draw a line from the animals to the place where they live.

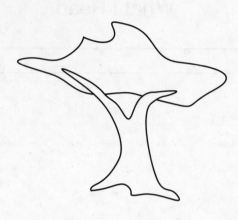

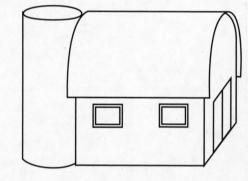

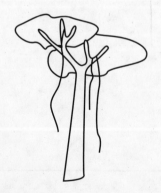

# A School of Fish

**1.** Color the fish that could not be real.

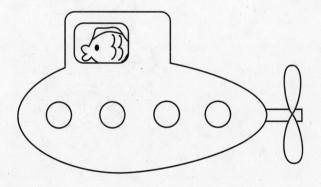

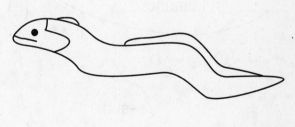

# Solve the Problems

**1.** Look at the pictures. **2.** Study the word problems. **3.** Write the root words on the lines below.

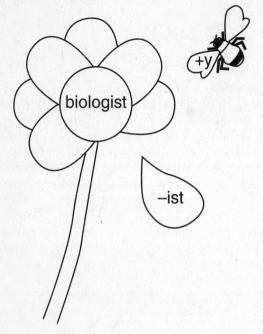

biologist – ist + y = _____     bucketful – ful = _____

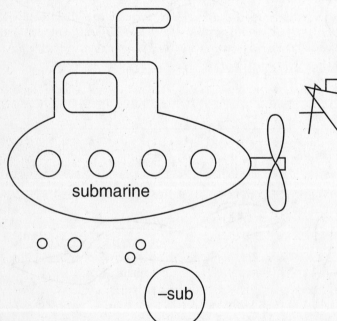

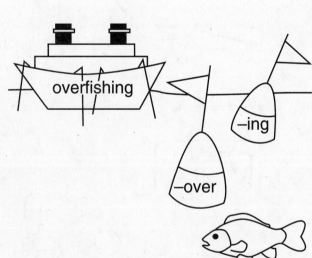

Submarine – sub = _____     overfishing – over – ing = _____

Written by Joanna Cole

## BUILD BACKGROUND FOR LANGUAGE SUPPORT

# I. FOCUS ON READING

## Focus on Skills

### Develop Visual Literacy

**OBJECTIVE:** Identify steps in a process

Tell students to close their eyes and visualize a fish. Then ask students to draw a fish. Have volunteers name fish parts (tail, scales, fins, eyes, mouth). Instruct the class to turn to the art on page 444. Explain to the class that Alexander Calder used various materials to create his sculpture *Fish*. Ask the class to name the materials they recognize in the sculpture (glass, wire, string) and to describe what purpose they serve (wire: body, tail, and eye of fish; scales: string and glass). Help students name the materials used to make the fish sculpture. As you discuss the artist's process, have students identify the order of the steps the artist might have gone through by raising one, two or three fingers. Model and give prompts such as: *The artist had to get glass and wire. Hold up your fingers to show if he did that first* (hold up one finger), *second* (hold up two fingers), *or last* (hold up three fingers). *Did the artist make the frame first* (hold up one finger), *second* (hold up two fingers), *or last* (hold up three fingers)? *Show me with your fingers. What did the artist do last?* Then list in order some steps for making this fish sculpture. Have students pantomime the steps in the process as you list them.

**TPR**

# II. READ THE LITERATURE

### Vocabulary

**VOCABULARY**
research
traditional
absorb
available
abandon
original

Introduce the words by reading the sentences on Teacher Chart 110. Emphasize the vocabulary word and repeat the underlined context clues. Ask volunteers to act out the context clues. Invite students to suggest definitions and use their definition to replace the vocabulary word in the sentence. Have students check to see if the new definition fits the underlined context clues.

Then print the vocabulary words on cards and guide students in the following activities to check comprehension. Hold up each word at the appropriate time. For example, display the word research, and ask: *Where do we go to do <u>research</u> for reports? Where do we find what we need to know?* Help students understand that research can be done in many ways. Then show a sponge absorbing a bit of water, and say: *Find something else in the room that can <u>absorb</u> water like this sponge.* Use body language and repetition as you give the following commands to encourage students to demonstrate understanding of the vocabulary words. If possible play a game similar to musical chairs using the following sentences as instructions for the game: Say: *Sit in your chair with your feet on the floor. This is the <u>traditional</u> way to sit in a chair. Now sit a different way. Sit the <u>traditional</u> way again.* Play music and say: *Walk around the room. And when the music stops sit in the closest <u>available</u> chair. When the music starts again <u>abandon</u> that chair and walk around again. Return to your original chair.*

## Evaluate Prior Knowledge

**CONCEPT**
how books are made

Display several nonfiction books. Lead students in a discussion of the process an author goes through to write a book. Ask them about their own experiences with the writing process: choosing and researching a topic, making an outline, writing a rough draft, revising, rewriting, and turning in a final paper. If possible, bring in pictures or props that illustrate these steps in the writing process, for example: someone doing research in the library, an outline, a rough draft of a report, and so on. Then help students relate these steps to how published books are made. Ask them to identify similarities and differences between student writers and published authors.

## Develop Oral Language

Have students work in small groups to dramatize the book-making process. Use prompts appropriate for students' linguistic level.

nonverbal prompt for active participation

• Preproduction: Model and say: *Find something in the room you can use to help you write a book. Show it to us. Find something else. Show us how you use it.*

one- or two-word response prompt

• Early production: *What is your book about? Do you know much about* (name of topic)*? Where can you go to learn more? What will you do next? Will you write a rough draft or a final copy first?*

prompt for short answers to higher-level thinking skills

• Speech emergence: *What is your book about? What will you do first? What kind of help or information will you need? Where can you go to find this? What will you do after you write a rough draft?*

prompt for detailed answers to higher-level thinking skills

• Intermediate fluency: *Tell us about your book. Why did you choose that topic? What steps will you take to write the book? What will you do first, next, last? What do you think will be the most difficult part of making a book? What do you think will be the most fun? Why?*

# Guided Instruction

## Preview and Predict

Read the title with students. Explain that an autobiography is a story or book in which the author writes about her or his own life. Ask students if they have heard of Joanna Cole or the Magic School Bus books. If students are unfamiliar with these books, you may want to bring in some examples. Tell them that in this story Joanna Cole is writing about a special part of her life. Have students preview the story. Encourage them to use the illustrations to make predictions and to reinforce the concept of how books are made. Ask questions such as: *What part of Joanna Cole's life do you think she has written about in this story? Find a picture that shows Joanna Cole working. What is she doing? Now find another picture of her working. Is she doing something different? What? What might this tell us about how books are made? Point to a picture that shows something you think Joanna Cole has written about. Can you find something else she might have written about? What is it? How are these things the same? How are they different?* Now have students work with a partner to write questions they have about how books are made. Review the questions after reading the story to see whether they were answered or require further research.

**GRAPHIC ORGANIZER**
Blackline Master 73

## Objectives

• To practice identifying steps in a process
• To reinforce drawing conclusions
• To support cooperative learning

**Materials**

One copy of Blackline Master 73 per student pair; pencils

Go over the chart headings with students. Explain that they will record the steps Joanna Cole follows as she writes a book. As you read the story, stop frequently, and ask questions such as: *What did Ms. Cole do first? What did she do next?* Have students work with partners to number and write the steps in the left column. They can then write or draw a brief description of each step.

To reinforce the skill of drawing conclusions, have students review their charts, and then tell whether they think writing a book is easy or hard.

# III. BUILD SKILLS

## Comprehension

**REVIEW STEPS IN A PROCESS**
Blackline Master 74

**Objectives**
• To practice identifying steps in a process
• To encourage higher-level thinking skills
• To support hands-on learning

**Materials**

One copy of Blackline Master 74 per student; scissors; paste or glue

Read the heading "Writing a Book" together. Then help students identify what is happening in the picture. Invite pairs to cut out the pictures and paste them in the correct sequence in the numbered boxes. Each student can then use the pictures to describe the sequence of events.

**INFORMAL ASSESSMENT**

Direct students to page 450. After rereading the page, have students name some of the steps Joanna Cole goes through before she begins writing a draft.

## Comprehension

**REVIEW DISTINGUISH BETWEEN FACT AND NONFACT**
Blackline Master 75

**Objectives**
• To practice distinguishing between fact and nonfact
• To support creative thinking
• To reinforce use of picture clues

**Materials**

One copy of Blackline Master 75 per student; crayons; pencils

Explain to students that writers have many ideas about books they might write. Have them describe the ideas this writer has. Tell students to color the ideas that are make-believe. Encourage them to tell why the ideas are fantasy. Then have them write or draw pictures of some ideas they have for books. Call on volunteers to share their ideas with the others.

**INFORMAL ASSESSMENT**

Ask students to decide whether they think the story is fact or nonfact. Have them find an illustration or text to support their opinion. Call on students to share their opinions and supporting evidence.

# Vocabulary Strategy

## Objectives

• To practice applying prefixes to create new words
• To reinforce structural analysis
• To support vocabulary development

## Materials

One copy of Blackline Master 76 per student; scissors; paste or glue; pencils

Have students read the root words in the larger pictures. Then tell them to cut out the small pictures containing prefixes, and paste them in the larger pictures. They can write the new words on the lines. Invite each student to read the root word and new word to a partner.

**INFORMAL ASSESSMENT**

Have students turn to page 454. Challenge them to find a word with a prefix (research, disappeared, reemerge). Call on students to read the words they find. Then have them remove each prefix and identify the root words.

## Steps in a Process

| STEP | DESCRIPTION |
|------|-------------|
|      |             |
|      |             |
|      |             |
|      |             |
|      |             |
|      |             |

# Stepping Along

**1.** Cut out the pictures below. **2.** Paste them in the order that they would happen in real life.

## Writing a Book

**1.**

**2.**

**3.**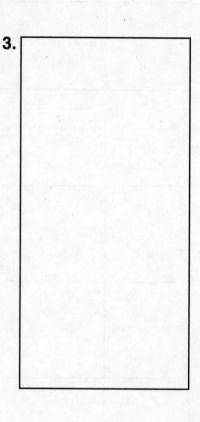

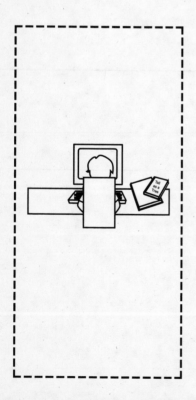

# Ideas

**1.** Color the pictures that show ideas for make-believe stories. **2.** Write your own ideas for make-believe stories on the lines below.

_____

_____

_____

# Missing Parts

**1.** Cut out the small pictures at the bottom of the page. **2.** Paste them on the large pictures. **3.** Write the new words on the lines below each large picture.

side

_____

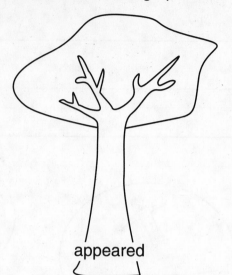

appeared

_____

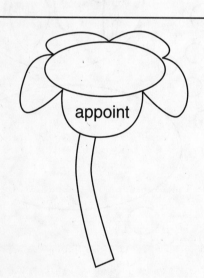

appoint

_____

to

_____

dis-

in-

in-

dis-

# EARTH'S FIRST CREATURES pp. 472A–481P

## BUILD BACKGROUND FOR LANGUAGE SUPPORT

# I. FOCUS ON READING

## Focus on Skills

**OBJECTIVE:** Compare and contrast

**TPR**

### Develop Visual Literacy

Have students turn to the painting on page 472. Ask students to raise their hands if they have seen similar paintings in a museum or in a book. Then point to the dinosaur in the water and ask: *Is this a dinosaur?* Point to the snails and ask: *Are these snails?* Then ask students: *What other animals are in the picture?* Encourage students to compare and contrast elements in the painting by giving directives and prompts such as: *Touch the dinosaur in the water. Is it big or little? Touch an animal that is smaller than the dinosaur. Can you point to one that is about the same size? Look at the dinosaur on land and the one in the water. Stand up if you see something about them that is the same. Show us what it is. Raise your hand if you see something that is different. Point to the things that are different.*

Have pairs draw or paint their own dinosaur scenes. When everyone is finished, display the pictures. Encourage students to compare and contrast the drawings. Ask: *How are these pictures alike? How are they different?*

# II. READ THE LITERATURE

### Vocabulary

**VOCABULARY**
microscope
ancestors
snout
spikes
weird
disaster

Print each vocabulary word on a flashcard. Bring the following pictures to class to give students a visual clue to the words:

*microscope:* A picture of a microscope.

*ancestors:* A black and white photo of a couple in the seventies.

*snout:* Bring in a picture of a dog or a cat and point to its nose.

*spikes:* Show a picture of the sole of a pair of golf or soccer shoes.

*weird:* Show a picture of an odd looking person or thing.

*disaster:* Use a photo of a natural disaster such as a tornado, earthquake or hurricane.

Display the flashcard as you show the pictures and say the vocabulary word. Then display the flashcard again for a word as you say it aloud and read the corresponding sentences from Teacher Chart 116. Have students turn back to the Visual Literacy painting on page 472–473. Ask the following questions: *Would you need a <u>microscope</u> to see these large animals? What kinds of animals would you look at with a <u>microscope</u>? Whose <u>ancestors</u> do you think these are?* (point to dolphin-like dinosaurs) *Which animal has a long, thin <u>snout</u>? What would the dinosaur in the water look like with sharp, pointy <u>spikes</u> on its back? Show how you would draw the <u>spikes</u>. What is <u>weird</u> about this bird-like dinosaur?* (point to pterodactyl catching a fish) *What makes it different than a bird? Would a natural <u>disaster</u> change the way these dinosaurs live? What kind of natural <u>disaster</u> could hurt these dinosaurs?*

Line the flashcards up on the chalkboard ledge in random order. Repeat the sentences, this time leaving out the vocabulary word. Ask pairs of students to come forward to select the correct flashcard.

## Evaluate Prior Knowledge

Bring in picture books and drawings of dinosaurs and other prehistoric creatures. Include several photos of prehistoric skeletons and fossils. Begin by showing pictures of skeletons. Explain that the skeletons are of creatures that lived long ago. Ask students what they can tell about each animal by looking at its skeleton. *What do you think it was? Was it big or small? Do you think it ate other animals?* Explain that we use bones and fossils to learn about prehistoric creatures like dinosaurs. Show the pictures of dinosaurs and have students tell what they know about them.

## Develop Oral Language

Give each student a picture. Ask them to show their pictures to the rest of the group one at a time. Develop language by giving prompts such as these:

nonverbal prompt for active
participation

• Preproduction: *Stand up and show us* (point to self and class) *your animal* (point to picture). *Show us how you think it moved* (dramatize walking). *Point to* (indicate other pictures of prehistoric animals and plants) *something it might have eaten* (dramatize eating).

one- or two-word response
prompt

• Early production: *Show us your animal. What is it? Is it big or little? What color is it? Do you think it walked, swam, or flew? Do you think it ate plants or animals?*

prompt for short answers to
higher-level thinking skills

• Speech emergence: *What is your animal? Describe it to us. How do you think it moved? What do you think it ate? Why do you think this?*

prompt for detailed answers to
higher-level thinking skills

• Intermediate fluency: *Describe your animal. Tell us how you think it lived. Explain why you think this. How did scientists figure out what this animal was like? Compare this animal with others you have seen. How are they the same? How are they different?*

# Guided Instruction

## Preview and Predict

Read the title with students. Explain that the word creatures in the title means animals. Ask students what they think the story will be about. As you preview the stories pictures with the class reinforce their comprehension of a prehistoric creature. Ask questions such as: *Do you think these were real animals or make-believe animals? Why do you think that? Point to an animal that is like an animal alive today. How are they the same? How are they different? Touch an animal that looks make-believe. What makes it look like it is not real? Look at the animals on page 475. How do you think they ate? How do you think they moved? Why do you think this?* Then have students work with a partner to identify things they hope to learn from reading the article. Record these on a chart and review them after students have completed the reading.

## Objectives

• To practice comparing and contrasting
• To practice distinguishing fact from nonfact
• To support cooperative learning

### Materials

One copy of Blackline Master 77 per two students; pencils

Have students read the chart headings. Tell them they will be looking for ways Cambrian creatures and creatures of today are alike and different. Stop reading after each page and have students work with partners to list similarities and differences between specific Cambrian creatures and creatures of today. Students needing extra language support can draw pictures or copy phrases from the board.

To reinforce the skill of distinguishing fact from nonfact, have students review their completed charts to determine whether each statement is a fact or a nonfact. Encourage them to explain their answers.

# III. BUILD SKILLS

## Comprehension

**REVIEW STEPS IN A PROCESS**
Blackline Master 78

### Objectives
- To practice identifying steps in a process
- To reinforce story details
- To support hands on learning

### Materials

One copy of Blackline Master 78 per student; scissors; paste or glue

Go over the pictures with students. Help them identify the progression from animals of long ago to animals of today. Have pairs cut out the puzzle pieces, turn them face down, and mix them up. Then have them turn the pieces face up and try to fit them together in the correct order. Once the order is intact, encourage pairs to describe what is happening in each step.

**INFORMAL ASSESSMENT**

Have students find an illustration in the story that shows steps in a process. Ask them to tell what process the illustration depicts.

## Vocabulary Strategy

**REVIEW PREFIXES**
Blackline Master 79

### Objectives
- To identify the prefixes *dis-* and *in-*
- To practice adding prefixes to create new words
- To reinforce structural analysis
- To support hands-on learning

### Materials

One copy of Blackline Master 79 per student; scissors; paste or glue; pencils

Have students read the prefixes in the two octopuses and the root words below. Help them with any unfamiliar words. Then tell them to cut out each word and paste it on the octopus with the appropriate prefix to create a new word. Have students write the words they create on the lines below each octopus. Then have them read the new words to a partner.

**INFORMAL ASSESSMENT**

Direct students to page 476. Challenge them to find words with the prefixes *in-* and *dis-*. (discovered, invisible) Call on volunteers to read the words they found. Then have students turn to page 475. Read aloud the first sentence of the second paragraph: *Then BAM!—animals appeared.* Ask students what would happen to the sentence if they added the prefix *dis-* to the word *appeared.*

# Vocabulary Strategy

**REVIEW ROOT WORDS**
Blackline Master 80

## Objectives
• To practice finding root words
• To reinforce structural analysis
• To support vocabulary development

## Materials

One copy of Blackline Master 80 per student; pencils

Have students read each word with affixes. Help them with any unfamiliar words. Then tell them to subtract affixes as shown, and add letters as indicated to arrive at the root words. Have them write each root word on the appropriate line and then read it aloud.

**INFORMAL ASSESSMENT**

Have students work in small groups. Assign each group a page from the story. Challenge them to find words that have prefixes or suffixes and remove the affixes to find the root words. Have them share their root words with the rest of the group.

# Compare and Contrast

| Similarities | Differences |
|---|---|
| | |

# Timeline

**1.** Cut out the puzzle pieces. **2.** Paste them together.

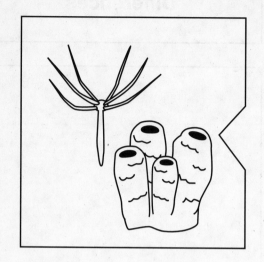

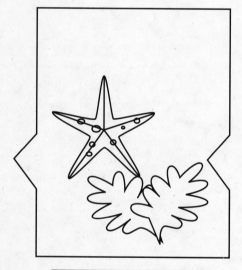

# Animal Arms

**1.** Cut out the words below. **2.** Paste the words on the octopus that can make it a new word. **3.** Write the new words on the lines.

_____   _____

_____   _____

_____   _____

_____   _____

| cover | visible |
| agree | complete |
| connect | put |
| please | side |

# Word Parts

**1.** Add or subtract word parts to find the root word. **2.** Write the root words on the lines.

overfishing

-over
-ing _____

_____

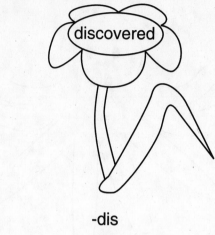

discovered

-dis
-ed _____

_____

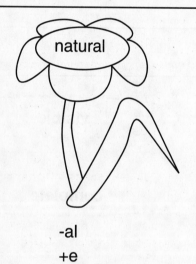

natural

-al
+e _____

_____

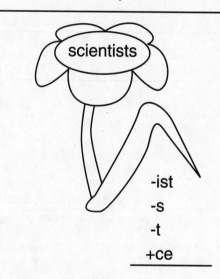

scientists

-ist
-s
-t
+ce _____

_____

# THE FOX AND THE GUINEA PIG pp. 486A–515P

Illustrated by Kevin Hawkes  Translated by Mary Ann Newman

## BUILD BACKGROUND FOR LANGUAGE SUPPORT

# I. FOCUS ON READING

## Focus on Skills

### Develop Visual Literacy

**OBJECTIVE:** Identify sequence of events

Ask students to stand up and form a line. Then point to a student at the beginning of the line and say. Ask students: *Who comes first? Who comes next?* Then ask students to sit down. Explain that a sequence is an order, similar to the order of the line they just formed. Then ask students to identify what you just had them do. Guide them to see that first, you asked them to stand up and form a line. Then, you asked students to identify who was first in line, who was next in line, and so on. Finally, you had students sit down. Then have students turn their attention to the picture *A Snow Leopard Stalking Ovis Polii.* Ask students to identify the animals in the picture. Say: *Touch the sheep. How do you think they feel? Do you think they were afraid before or after they saw the snow leopard?* Help students dramatize the sequence of events by giving prompts such as: *Show us what you think the sheep looked like before they saw the snow leopard. Now show what they look like when they see the snow leopard. What will the snow leopard do now? What will the sheep do after that?* After the dramatization, encourage students to identify the beginning, middle, and end of their story. Write the sequence of events on the chalkboard

**TPR**

# II. READ THE LITERATURE

## Vocabulary

**VOCABULARY**
amazement
strewn
destroyed
eldest
fowl
stake

Introduce the vocabulary words by reading the sentences on Teacher Chart 122. Emphasize the vocabulary word and repeat the underlined context clues. Ask volunteers to act out the context clues. For instance, have students cluck like chickens for *fowl*, and have them tear up a piece of paper to show *destroyed*. Invite students to suggest definitions and use their definition to replace the vocabulary word in the sentence. Have students check to see if the new definition fits the underlined context clues. Then pose questions using the new words and words with contrasting meanings. For example, ask: *Which sounds more correct: The house was destroyed by the twister; The house was built by the twister? When clothes are strewn around the room, are they all over the room or just in one place? Is the eldest daughter older or younger than her sisters? Which is a fowl, a cow or a chicken? Is someone surprised or bored when they feel amazement? Is a stake used to hold something in place or to help it move around?* Finally, have students gather in small groups and assign each group a vocabulary word. Tell students to write a context sentence using the vocabulary word and to create a drawing to accompany the sentence. Have each group take turns presenting the sentence and drawing to the rest of the class.

### Evaluate Prior Knowledge

**CONCEPT**
using your wits

Explain to students that the term "using your wits" means to think fast or come up with a good idea for solving a problem. Demonstrate "using your wits" by telling them that today is your mother's birthday and you forgot to get her a gift. Have students "use their wits" to come up with things you might do, such as call her, make her something, or surprise her and take her out for ice cream. Ask volunteers to tell about a time they "used their wits" to solve a problem.

---

## Develop Oral Language

Have students work in small groups. Give each group a situation to dramatize in which they need to use their wits. For example: you're at home and a fire breaks out; your cat is stuck in a tree; you and a friend get lost on a hike; and so on. Use prompts appropriate for students' linguistic level.

nonverbal prompt for active participation

- Preproduction: *Show us* (Point to self and class) *what you* (point to student) *would do if there were a fire* (show a picture of fire and indicate classroom). *Show us how you would be safe* (wipe brow in gesture of relief).

one- or two-word response prompt

- Early production: *If your cat were stuck in a tree, what would you do? Would you get help? Would you climb the tree? Would you try to get the cat to come down? How would you do that?*

prompt for short answers to higher-level thinking skills

- Speech emergence: *What is the problem you have to solve? How will you solve it?*

prompt for detailed answers to higher-level thinking skills

- Intermediate fluency: *What is the problem? What will you try first? What if that doesn't work? Why would you do that? What other ways could the problem be solved?*

# Guided Instruction

### Preview and Predict

Tell students this story is about a very clever animal that uses its wits to get out of trouble. Read the title, and have students identify the fox and the guinea pig in the illustrations. Skim through the story, using the illustrations to reinforce the concept of using your wits and to encourage predictions. Ask questions such as: *Which animal do you think uses its wits? Why do you think this? How do you think the guinea pig gets the fox to untie him? What could the guinea pig be doing with the big rock? What do you think the fox is doing with it? How do you think the guinea pig might be tricking the fox? What do you think the fox is afraid of? What might happen after the fox is buried?* Encourage students to talk about reasons to read the story. For example, they might want to learn why the guinea pig is tied up, what the guinea pig says to the fox, or why the fox is buried.

**GRAPHIC ORGANIZER**
Blackline Master 81

### Objectives

- To practice determining a sequence of events
- To reinforce understanding of main events in a story

### Materials

One copy of Blackline Master 81 per two students; pencils

Tell students that they will keep track of the events in the story by recording them on the Sequence of Events chart. Read the chart heading with students. Then read the story, stopping after main events, so that partners can record them in the boxes. For example, after reading page 491, have students write what Don Emicho does when he realizes something has been in his alfalfa. After reading page 493, have students record what happens after Don Emicho sets his trap. Encourage students to record the events they think are most important to the story.

As an alternate method for reviewing sequence, write an unordered list of important story events on the board. Have partners copy the phrases onto their charts in the correct order.

# III. BUILD SKILLS

## Comprehension

### REVIEW SEQUENCE OF EVENTS
Blackline Master 82

**Objectives**
- To identify the sequence of events in a story
- To recall main events

**Materials**

One copy of Blackline Master 82 per student; scissors; paste or glue; pencils

Review the worksheet with students, helping them read the sentences at the top of the page. Have students tell what is happening in each picture. Have students cut out the sentences and paste them under the pictures they describe. Have them place one sentence in an empty box. Then have students draw a picture in the empty box to illustrate the sentence under it.

**INFORMAL ASSESSMENT**

Have students work in small groups. Assign each team one of the three situations in which the guinea pig tricked the fox. Have the groups determine the sequence of events for that particular situation and share them with the rest of the group.

## Comprehension

### REVIEW SUMMARIZING
Blackline Master 83

**Objectives**
- To make inferences about character and setting
- To reinforce understanding of story elements
- To support higher-level thinking skills

**Materials**

One copy of Blackline Master 83 per student; pencils

Go over the page with students, helping them read any unfamiliar words in the instructions. Then have students draw pictures and write a word or short phrase to describe how the story characters felt in the different situations. Encourage students to go back to the appropriate pages in the story to help them make their inferences. Have them share their responses with a partner.

**INFORMAL ASSESSMENT**

Direct students to page 497. Ask: *How do you think the fox feels about being tied up?* Then have students turn to page 499, and tell how the fox felt when Don Emicho found him. Encourage students to give reasons for their answers.

# Vocabulary Strategy

**REVIEW CONTEXT CLUES**
Blackline Master 84

## Objectives

- To use context clues
- To reinforce story vocabulary
- To support cooperative learning

## Materials

One copy of Blackline Master 84 per two students; scissors

Help students read the words in the right column. Explain that each word describes something about one of the pictures in the left column. Have students cut out the words and pictures. Invite them to work with partners to match each picture with the word that tells something about it. Encourage students to use each word in a sentence.

**INFORMAL ASSESSMENT**

Have students reread page 506. Ask them to find the two words that describe how the fox is feeling. (perturbed and frightened) Ask students to use context clues to figure out the meaning of perturbed

# Determining Sequence of Events

## Sequence of Events

```
┌─────────────────────────────────────────────┐
│                                               │
│                                               │
└─────────────────────────────────────────────┘
                      │
                      ▼
┌─────────────────────────────────────────────┐
│                                               │
│                                               │
└─────────────────────────────────────────────┘
                      │
                      ▼
┌─────────────────────────────────────────────┐
│                                               │
│                                               │
└─────────────────────────────────────────────┘
                      │
                      ▼
┌─────────────────────────────────────────────┐
│                                               │
│                                               │
└─────────────────────────────────────────────┘
                      │
                      ▼
┌─────────────────────────────────────────────┐
│                                               │
│                                               │
└─────────────────────────────────────────────┘
                      │
                      ▼
┌─────────────────────────────────────────────┐
│                                               │
│                                               │
└─────────────────────────────────────────────┘
                      │
                      ▼
┌─────────────────────────────────────────────┐
│                                               │
│                                               │
└─────────────────────────────────────────────┘
```

Name_____ Date_____

# What Happened When?

1. Cut out the sentences. 2. Paste them in order under the drawing they match.
3. Draw the missing picture.

> Guinea pig buries fox.
>
> Farmer traps guinea pig.
>
> Farmer finds destroyed patch.
>
> Fox holds up rock.
>
> Guinea pig ties up fox.

# What Do You Think?

**1.** Write and draw to tell how the farmer felt at the beginning of the story.

**2.** Write and draw to tell how the guinea pig felt about being tied to the tree.

**3.** Write and draw to tell how the guinea pig felt at the end of the story.

# Word Game

**1.** Cut out the pictures and words below. **2.** Match each word to a picture it defines.

| | |
|---|---|
| | **strewn** |
| | **fowl** |
| | **amazement** |
| | **eldest** |
| | **destroyed** |
| | **stake** |

# MOM'S BEST FRIEND pp. 516A–535P

Written by Sally Hobart Alexander  Photographs by George Ancona

## BUILD BACKGROUND FOR LANGUAGE SUPPORT

## I. FOCUS ON READING

### Focus on Skills

**OBJECTIVE:** Distinguish between important and unimportant information

**TPR**

### Develop Visual Literacy

Have students look at the painting on page 516. Explain that the painting is a mural created by people living in Santa Fe, New Mexico. As students look at the picture, encourage them to think about the people who painted the mural. Encourage them to try to identify what might be important to these people. Say: *Touch the tree in the picture. Do you think it is special or important to the people in that community? Why do you think that? Touch the land in the picture. Raise your hand if it looks hot and dry. How might that be important? Follow the river with your finger. How can you tell it is important to these people? Why would a river be important?* Then organize the class into groups of four to five students. Give each group a large piece of butcher paper and have them create a mural that tells about their community. Ask them to include both important and unimportant information in their murals. Have each group share its completed mural with the class. Encourage students to guess which elements in each mural are important or unimportant and tell why.

## II. READ THE LITERATURE

### Vocabulary

**VOCABULARY**
errands
instinct
memorizing
sirens
clippers
relieved

Write the vocabulary words on cards, and place them on the ledge of the chalkboard. Develop meaning for each word by demonstrating the following activities. Use body language and props in your demonstration. Point to the appropriate word card each time a word is mentioned. Begin by saying: *Sometimes I do errands like go to the post office or the grocery store. Stand up and tell us what errands you do. Act out an errand you do often. A dog's instinct is to chase cats. Pretend you are a dog and you see a cat. Act out this instinct.* Place four or five objects on the table. Then say: *Spend one minute memorizing the things on this table. Now close your eyes and tell us everything you remember. Fire trucks, ambulances and police cars have sirens to tell other cars to get out of their way. Make a sound like a siren.* Show several clippers: nail, garden, and so forth. *These are clippers. Pick up one and tell us what you think it is for. I thought I had lost my wallet. I was relieved when I found it. Show how you look when you feel relieved.* Then have students form small groups and assign each group a vocabulary word. Have students work together to form a definition for their word. Then ask groups to switch words and repeat the process. Continue until each group has written a definition for each word. Finally, say each word and have groups present their definitions. Ask students to vote on which definition they think is best.

### Evaluate Prior Knowledge

**CONCEPT**
animals that help people

Bring in pictures of animals helping people in various situations. Some examples may be: dogs helping blind or otherwise disabled people, Saint Bernards helping people in snowstorms, police dogs helping sniff for drugs, dolphins helping people at sea, horses or other animals helping farmers plow, and so on. Ask students what all the pictures have in common. If necessary, ask what the animals are doing in each picture. Discuss the pictures with students, guiding them to see the many ways animals help people. Encourage them to think of other ways animals help us.

## Develop Oral Language

Tell students to choose or draw a picture of an animal that they would like to have help them. Have them tell or show the class how this animal would help them and why they would want it to. Use prompts such as:

nonverbal prompt for active participation

• **Preproduction:** *Show us* (point to self and class) *which animal you chose* (point to picture). *Show us what a* (point to and name animal) *could do for you* (point to student).

one- or two-word response prompt

• **Early production:** *What is the name of your animal? Is it big or little? Can it help you do things? What will it help you do? Have you seen this animal before? Is it friendly?*

prompt for short answers to higher-level thinking skills

• **Speech emergence:** *What animal would you like to help you? What does it look like? Where does it live? How would you like a* (name of animal) *to help you? Why? Has it helped other people? What else do you know about this animal?*

prompt for detailed answers to higher-level thinking skills

• **Intermediate fluency:** *Tell us about the animal you chose. How would you like it to help you? Why? What else do you think it could do? How has it helped other people? Would you have to train it? How would you do that?*

## Guided Instruction

### Preview and Predict

Tell students that this story is about Sally Hobart Alexander, a woman who is blind and uses a guide dog. Read the title, author, and photographer names. Point out that the woman on the title page is the author. Preview the story with students, using the photographs to reinforce the concept of animals that help people. Encourage students to make predictions about the story. Ask questions such as: *Look at the dog on the first page. What is it wearing that is special? What do you think the harness is for? Why do you think Sally is walking with a cane? What else could she use to help her cross the street? How do you think the dog in these pictures helps Sally? How do you think Sally feels about her dog? What makes you think that? How do you think the dog guide and the family feel about each other? Who do you think Mom's best friend is?* Then have students discuss reasons to read the selection. (Possible answers: to find out the many ways the dog helps Sally; to learn more about dog guides and how they are trained to help people; to find out what it is like to be blind.)

**GRAPHIC ORGANIZER**
Blackline Master 85

### Objectives

• To distinguish between important and unimportant information
• To support higher-level thinking skills

### Materials

One copy of Blackline Master 85 per two students; pencils

Review the chart with students. Explain that the main idea of a story is the most important thing about the story, or what the story is about. After reading page 520, stop and ask students what they think the main idea of the story is. (The story will be about Mom getting a new guide dog.) Have students write this in the box labeled *Main Idea* on their charts. Then write the following statements on the chalkboard: *Mom's dog guide, Marit, died. My brother gave me a rabbit. Mom lost her favorite way of traveling when Marit died. Marit used to steal pizza from the counter.* Then ask students: *Which of the following statements supports the main idea? Which of the following statements are unimportant.* Guide students to see that the first and third statements are important because they tell the reader why Mom decided to get a new guide dog. The other statements are unimportant because they do not support the main idea. As you read the story, stop periodically to ask students if specific details they read are important or unimportant to the story. Help them record on their charts the important details that support the main idea. When the charts are complete, invite volunteers to share theirs with the class.

# III. BUILD SKILLS

## Comprehension

**REVIEW IMPORTANT
AND UNIMPORTANT
INFORMATION**
Blackline Master 86

### Objectives
• To identify a main idea
• To find important information to support the main idea
• To support hands-on learning

### Materials
One copy of Blackline Master 86 per student; scissors; paper; glue or paste

Help students read the sentences in the puzzle pieces. Discuss the sentences that describe important details from the story. Explain that the pieces have important details on them and can be put together to make the picture of the dog that is shown in the top left corner. Have students cut out the puzzle pieces. Have them glue or paste the important pieces together on a piece of paper to complete the puzzle.

**INFORMAL ASSESSMENT**

Direct students to page 522. Have them skim the page, identifying details that are important to the story as well as those that are not so important. Invite volunteers to explain why certain details are important and others are unimportant. Repeat with other pages.

## Comprehension

**REVIEW MAKE
INFERENCES**
Blackline Master 87

### Objectives
• To make inferences about a character
• To encourage higher-level thinking skills

### Materials
One copy of Blackline Master 87 per student; scissors

Tell students that they can often learn more about a story from other things they already know. Go over the column headings together. Explain that the left column contains facts from the story and the right column explains inferences made from those facts. Have students read the sentences in each column. Help them with any unfamiliar words. Then tell students to cut out each square and match a fact from the story with an inference that can be made from that fact. Invite students to share their results with a partner.

**INFORMAL ASSESSMENT**

Have students turn to page 524 and read the last paragraph. Ask them to tell how they think the narrator is feeling. Encourage them to give reasons to support their answers.

**INTRODUCE FIGURATIVE LANGUAGE**
Blackline Master 88

### Objectives
• To learn how to recognize similes and metaphors
• To create their own similes and metaphors

### Materials

One copy of Blackline Master 88 per student; pencils

Explain that sometimes an author describes something by comparing it to something else. Look at the page with students. Help students read figurative language in speech bubbles. In the space provided, have students write in their own words what they think is meant by each sentence. Invite students to share their interpretations with the rest of the class.

**INFORMAL ASSESSMENT**

Direct students to page 526. Have them read the letter Leslie wrote to her mom. Ask them to say what they think the sentence *The house misses you* means. Then have them read the letter Mom wrote back. Challenge them to tell what the sentence, *We'll be home to "hound" you on Thursday,* means.

# Important and Unimportant Information

Main Idea:

# The Important Parts

**1.** Cut out the pieces below along the dotted lines. **2.** Make a dog with the six pieces that tell you important parts of the story.

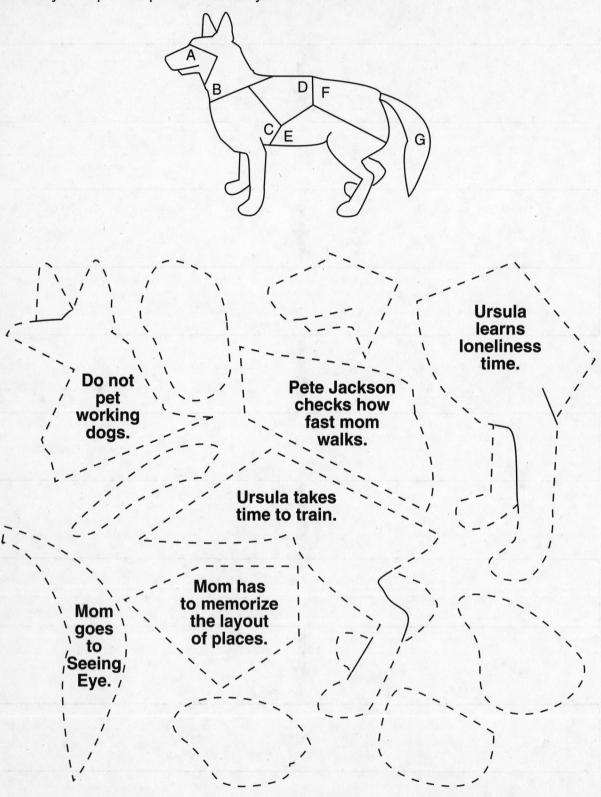

**Ursula learns loneliness time.**

**Do not pet working dogs.**

**Pete Jackson checks how fast mom walks.**

**Ursula takes time to train.**

**Mom has to memorize the layout of places.**

**Mom goes to Seeing Eye.**

# Learn From What You Know

**1.** Cut out each section. **2.** Match the sentences from the left side with the corresponding sentences from the right side.

| What We Know | What We Learn |
|---|---|
| In a month, Ursula emptied her food bowl every time. | Ursula liked me. |
| I wrote a braille letter. | Ursula got used to living with us. |
| Ursula sprang up on me. | Mom reads braille. |

# What Do You Mean?

**1.** Read the sentences below. Using your own words write what you think each statement means.

I will have grown four more feet.

_____

_____

I made Ursula my shadow.

_____

_____

_____

Ursula needs to start thinking tall.

_____

_____

## BUILD BACKGROUND FOR LANGUAGE SUPPORT

# I. FOCUS ON READING

## Focus on Skills

**OBJECTIVE:** To predict story events

**TPR**

### Develop Visual Literacy

Invite students to play a quick game of tic-tac-toe with a partner (best two out of three). Before they begin, have partners make a prediction about who will win each game. Encourage students to compare their predictions with the actual outcome of the game. Then invite students to look at the picture. Use prompts such as the following to encourage students to make predictions about what they see. *Point to the most important part of the painting. The boys are playing chess. Touch the boy you think will win the game. Show us how he will look when he wins. Point to the boy you think will lose. Show us what he might do next. Show us what you think the women will do when the game is over.*

# II. READ THE LITERATURE

### Vocabulary

**VOCABULARY**
celebration
attendants
knowledge
awkwardly
spice
released

Introduce the words by reading the sentences on Teacher Chart 134. Emphasize the vocabulary word and repeat the underlined context clues. Ask volunteers to act out the context clues. Encourage students to brainstorm definitions and use their definitions to replace the vocabulary word in the sentence. Have students check to see if the new definition fits the underlined context clues.

Write the vocabulary words on cards. Show the cards as you give the following prompts and suggestions to check comprehension. Use body language and modeling to help students with understanding.

Say: *A celebration is a festival or party.* Show a picture of a celebration, and say: *This is a celebration. Now you show or tell us about a celebration you have been to. A queen or king has many attendants who do things for them.* Show a picture from a fairy-tale book of a queen or king with attendants. Identify the attendants, and say: *Have one person in your group be a queen or king, and the others pretend to be attendants. Show us what attendants might do.* Point to your head, and say: *If you have knowledge about something, it means you know about it.* Point to something students know you are well-versed in, and say, for example: *I have a great deal of knowledge about dinosaurs. Tell us what you have knowledge of.* Hold a stack of books awkwardly, pretending to nearly drop them. Say: *I am carrying this stack of books awkwardly. Show how you would lift a chair awkwardly.* Hold a jar of cinnamon, and say: *Cinnamon is a spice; it is used to make food taste better. Name a spice you've tasted.* Hold a balloon and let it go. Say: *I released the balloon. When something is released, it means it is let go. Show what you do when you are released from school.*

## Evaluate Prior Knowledge

Pretend with students that you are planning a class party. Ask them to figure out how many cups of juice you will need for each student to have one. Then ask how many cookies will be needed for each student to have two. Encourage students to explain how they arrived at their answers. Tell them that they just used math to solve some problems. Ask them to tell about other times they have used math to solve problems.

Tell students they will be solving another problem with math. Pretend that one of their neighbors has put up a sign for kittens for sale. However, she only wants to sell them in pairs. Each kitten costs $5.00. In addition, the shots for each kitten will cost $25.00. Each kitten will eat $3.00 worth of food a week. The neighbor has offered to give you a week's supply of food free for each kitten you buy. Have students draw a picture of the kittens for sale, including the price of the kittens. Also include in the picture, the vet and the pet store, each displaying signs with the prices of shots and food, respectively.

## Develop Oral Language

nonverbal prompt for active participation

- Preproduction: *Point to the kittens. Show us how much you will have to pay your neighbor for two kittens. How much will you have to pay your neighbor for four kittens? Can you show us how you figured this out?*

one- or two-word response prompt

- Early production: *Tell us how much it will cost you to buy two kittens from your neighbor. How much will shots cost for both kittens? How much is the total of the price of the kittens and their shots? Show us how you figured this out?*

prompt for short answers to higher-level thinking skills

- Speech emergence: *If there are four weeks in a month, how much would a month's worth of food cost for two kittens? If your neighbor gives you one week's supply of food free for each kitten, how much will you save? Tell us if you used multiplication, subtraction, division, or addition to solve the problems.*

prompt for detailed answers to higher-level thinking skills

- Intermediate fluency: *What is the total cost of two kittens, their shots, and a month's supply of food, with one week free food for each kitten? Write the equations you used to figure this out on the chalkboard. If you only have $70 to spend this month, can you afford both kittens? How does using math help you solve problems?*

# Guided Instruction

## Preview and Predict

Read with students the title and subtitle. Explain that long ago the kings of India were known as Rajahs. Ask what students think a "mathematical folktale" refers to. Preview the story together, using the illustrations to reinforce the concept of using math to solve problems and to establish details about the rural Indian setting and the characters. Ask questions such as: *Who do you think this story is about? What can you tell about this girl? Why do you think the elephants are carrying all the rice out of the village? How do you think the villagers feel? Look at the rice on the chessboard. Count the grains of rice in the first three squares. Do you notice a pattern? What do you think will happen next?* Encourage students to talk about reasons for reading the selection. For example, they might say they want to find out what the girl does, to learn what happens to the Rajah's rice, or to see how math is used in the story.

GRAPHIC ORGANIZER
Blackline Master 89

## Objectives

- To make predictions
- To make inferences

**Materials**

One copy of Blackline Master 89 per student pair; pencils

Before reading the story, go over the chart headings with students. As you read, stop periodically and have students discuss with their partners what they think will happen. Students should write these predictions in the left-hand column on their charts. Make sure to provide opportunities for students to confirm or revise their predictions in the column labeled *What Happened*.

To reinforce the skill of making inferences, have students use their completed charts to tell what kind of person they think Chandra is.

# III. BUILD SKILLS

## Comprehension

**REVIEW MAKE PREDICTIONS**
Blackline Master 90

**Objectives**
• To review making predictions
• To encourage higher-level thinking skills

**Materials**

One copy of Blackline Master 90 per group; pencils

Have students work in small groups. Go over the column headings on the page. As you read the story, have students stop at important points and discuss in their groups what they think will happen next. They should list important story details in the first column and their predictions in the second column. When they are able to either confirm or revise their predictions, they should write what actually happened in the third column. Encourage group members to compare their predictions with what actually occurred.

**INFORMAL ASSESSMENT**

Have students turn to page 561. Ask them to predict what will happen next. Encourage them to give reasons to support their predictions.

## Comprehension

**REVIEW MAKE INFERENCES**
Blackline Master 91

**Objectives**
• To make inferences
• To reinforce understanding of story details

**Materials**

One copy of Blackline Master 91 per student; pencils

Explain to students that they can use their own experiences, as well as clues from the text, to make inferences about what is happening in a story. Review the worksheet with students. Help students read the first statement and the two sentences connected to it by arrows. Have students decide which arrow points to the sentence that seems true to that statement. Ask them to circle the sentence they feel is true. Encourage students to explain their answers. Repeat with the other statements and sentences on the page.

**INFORMAL ASSESSMENT**

Direct students to page 542. Have them read the page and then tell what kind of a person the Rajah is. Encourage them to give reasons to support their answers.

# Vocabulary Strategy

**REVIEW CONTEXT CLUES**
Blackline Master 92

## Objectives
• To review context clues
• To reinforce vocabulary

## Materials

One copy of Blackline Master 92 per student; pencils

Review the vocabulary words at the top of the page. Then read the paragraph with students. Stop at each blank and have students select the correct word and write it on the line. When all the blanks have been filled, have students reread the paragraph with a partner. Then have them illustrate the story in the box.

**INFORMAL ASSESSMENT**

Write the first sentence from page 558 on the board. Underline the word *collapsed*. Have students read the sentence and tell what they think *collapsed* means. Encourage them to use clues in the illustration as well as the words in the sentence to figure out the meaning of this word. Then have students turn to p. 540. Point out the words *egrets*. Ask students to tell what they think *egrets* are. Have them support their answer with clues from the illustration and text.

Name_______________________________ Date_______________

## Make Predictions

| Prediction | What Happened |
| --- | --- |
| | |

# What Will Happen?

**1.** List important points under the "Story Clue" column as you read the story. Then write your predictions in the "What I Think Will Happen" column. **2.** As you continue to read, write what actually happened in the last column.

| | Story Clue | What I Think Will Happen | What Actually Happened |
|---|---|---|---|
| **1.** | | | |
| **2.** | | | |
| **3.** | | | |
| **4.** | | | |

# What Does It Tell You?

**1.** Read the sentences in both columns. **2.** Circle the sentences in the right column that are true.

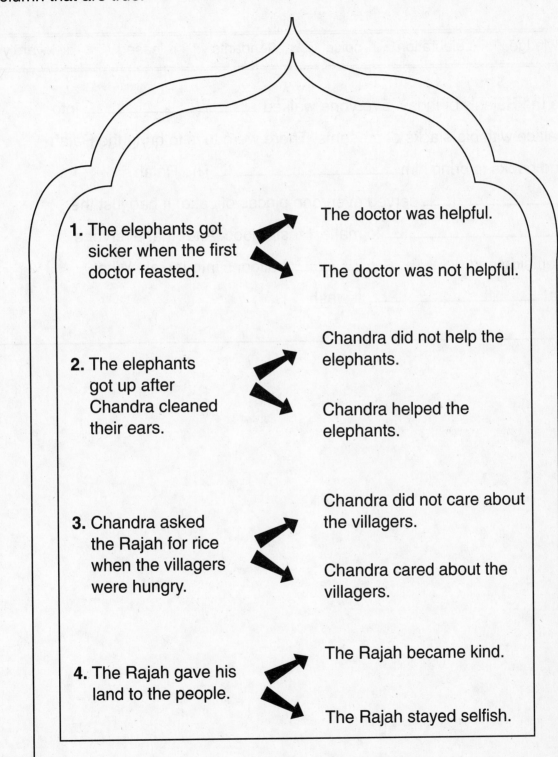

**1.** The elephants got sicker when the first doctor feasted.

The doctor was helpful.

The doctor was not helpful.

**2.** The elephants got up after Chandra cleaned their ears.

Chandra did not help the elephants.

Chandra helped the elephants.

**3.** Chandra asked the Rajah for rice when the villagers were hungry.

Chandra did not care about the villagers.

Chandra cared about the villagers.

**4.** The Rajah gave his land to the people.

The Rajah became kind.

The Rajah stayed selfish.

# Finish The Story

**1.** Read the story. **2.** Write the words in the blanks to finish the story. **3.** Draw a picture of the Rajah's birthday party in the box below.

| knowledge | celebration | spice | attendants | released | awkwardly |

It was the Rajah's birthday. Everyone walked _____ into the palace with big stacks of presents. There were toys to bring the Rajah joy and books to bring him _____. The Rajah's _____ served everyone pieces of cake. It had just the right _____ to make it taste good. After that everyone went outside and _____ balloons into the air. What a great _____ it was!

# YEH-SHEN pp. 568A–599P

### Retold by Ai-Ling Louie Illustrated by Ed Young

## BUILD BACKGROUND FOR LANGUAGE SUPPORT

# I. FOCUS ON READING

## Focus on Skills

### Develop Visual Literacy

**OBJECTIVE:** To sequence events

Review sequence of events with students. Ask students: *What is the first thing you will do when school is over today? Then what will you do? What is the last thing you will do before you go to sleep tonight?* Write student responses on the chalkboard. Then ask a volunteer to pantomime the different responses. Scramble the order of events and ask students: *What will happen if you do these things in a different order?* Then have students look at the collage entitled *Masters of Midnight*. Have students point to the different musicians and their instruments. Ask students: *Do the musicians look like they are in the middle of a song?* Explain that in many jazz songs, everyone in the band begins by playing together. Then individual musicians take turns playing by themselves. Encourage students to think about sequence of events by asking questions such as: *Are these musicians playing together or one at a time? Point to the musician you think will play by himself first. Point to the musician who may tell others when to play. Show us what you think will happen when the song is over. Show us what the musicians might do when the performance is over.*

**TPR**

# II. READ THE LITERATURE

### Vocabulary

**VOCABULARY**
beloved
desire
permit
heaved
marveled
bid

Write the vocabulary words on cards. Show each card as you briefly define the words, using body language, repetition, and appropriate props.

Say: *This is a picture of my beloved dog. I love her a lot. Tell us what is beloved by you.* Show a picture of someone receiving a birthday present. Say: *People often get presents on their birthdays. What do you desire for your birthday; what do you really want?* Hold up some chewing gum and say: *I do not permit gum in my class. Show something that I do permit you to do.* Show a picture of someone who has just heaved a heavy object. Say: *Show how the fisherman heaved this big fish into his boat.* Show a picture of some very small baby animals and say: *I marveled at how tiny the kittens were. What have you marveled at?* Wave, and say: *To bid you hello or good-bye is to say hello or good-bye. Bid your partner good-bye.*

Now have students work in small groups. Give each group a vocabulary card and have them dramatize the word on the card. The rest of the students can try to guess the word being acted out.

### Evaluate Prior Knowledge

**CONCEPT**
ancient China

Supply students with a globe and ask for a volunteer to show where China is located. Bring in pictures that depict ancient China. Try to include pictures of houses, people working, traditional dress, and so on. Explain that the story they will be reading takes place in China a time long ago. Display the pictures and help students name what they see. Encourage them to compare life today in the United States with life in ancient China.

### Develop Oral Language

Give each student a picture and have them dramatize or tell about it. Use prompts appropriate to students' linguistic levels. For example:

nonverbal prompt for active participation

- Preproduction: Model and say, for example: *Stand up and show us your picture. Point to the man. Show us what he is doing. Touch the young woman. Show us what she is doing.*

one- or two-word response prompt

- Early production: *What is your picture of? Are the homes big or small? What are they made of? Where are the people? What are they doing in the fields? What do we call people who grow crops?*

prompt for short answers to higher-level thinking skills

- Speech emergence: *Tell us about your picture. Who do you think this man is? How would you describe his clothing? How are his clothes different from clothing you see today in the United States?*

prompt for detailed answers to higher-level thinking skills

- Intermediate fluency: *Tell us about your picture. What are the people doing in the market? What kinds of things are being bought and sold? What don't you see in the market that you might see today? What does this tell you about life in ancient China?*

## Guided Instruction

### Preview and Predict

Tell students the story is a fairy tale about a girl in ancient China. Read the title and subtitle together, and have students identify Yeh-Shen. Explain the Cinderella story for those who are unfamiliar with it. Then have students preview the story by looking at the illustrations. Encourage students to point out elements in the pictures that show that the story takes place in ancient China. Ask questions such as: *Where do you think Yeh-Shen lives? What do you think Yeh-Shen is doing in this picture? How does her life seem different than yours? Do you think she has a happy life? Why do you think that? Where do you think Yeh-Shen got her beautiful clothes? Why do you think this fish is in the pictures?* Encourage students to talk about reasons for reading the story. For example, they might say they want to find out how Yeh-Shen is like or unlike other versions of Cinderella to learn about a Chinese fairy tale, or to find out what happens to Yeh-Shen.

**GRAPHIC ORGANIZER**
Blackline Master 93

### Objectives

- To identify a sequence of events
- To make inferences
- To support cooperative learning

### Materials

One copy of Blackline Master 93 per student pair; pencils

After reading the first two paragraphs of the story, ask students to record the main event in Yeh-Shen's life in the first box of the chart. As they finish the next paragraph have them write what happened after Yeh-Shen's mother died. Continue reading, but stop periodically to have students record the main story events in the order they occur. Students needing extra language support can be paired with a more fluent speaker or can copy from the chalkboard phrases generated by the group.

To reinforce the skill of making inferences, have students review their completed charts. Ask: *Based on what you know of Yeh-Shen and her life, what kind of a queen do you think she will make?*

# III. BUILD SKILLS

## Comprehension

**REVIEW SEQUENCE OF EVENTS**
Blackline Master 94

### Objectives
• To sequence events
• To distinguish between important and unimportant facts
• To support cooperative learning

### Materials
One copy of Blackline Master 94 per student pair; pencils

Have students discuss the story with a partner. Then help students read aloud the sentence in the first box on the sequence of events chart. Have students work together to write down in order the most important events from the story . When finished, students can compare their charts with others. Then invite students to chart the events of a day in their lives. Call on volunteers to share their personal sequence of events charts with the rest of the class. Discuss with students the importance of telling things in sequence.

**INFORMAL ASSESSMENT**

Direct students to page 586 and have them read the first paragraph. Ask them to give the sequence of events that led to the king receiving Yeh-Shen's slipper.

## Comprehension

**REVIEW MAKE PREDICTIONS**
Blackline Master 95

### Objectives
• To make predictions
• To reinforce understanding of story details
• To encourage higher-level thinking skills

### Materials
One copy of Blackline Master 95 per student; crayons; pencils

Have students discuss what is happening in each picture, and read the labels below them. Tell students to color the picture that shows what they think will happen to Yeh-Shen after she marries the king. Encourage students to give reasons to support their predictions. Challenge students to write, draw pictures, or tell a story about what happens next to Yeh-Shen.

**INFORMAL ASSESSMENT**

Have students turn to p. 584 and reread the first paragraph. Then ask: *What do you think the stepmother will do if she sees Yeh-Shen at the banquet?*

# Vocabulary Strategy

**REVIEW FIGURATIVE LANGUAGE**
Blackline Master 96

## Objectives
• To identify and use figurative language
• To encourage creative thinking
• To support vocabulary development

## Materials

One copy of Blackline Master 96 per student; crayons; pencils

Read the first sentence with students. Have them draw a picture to illustrate the sentence. Then have them write on the line what they think the figurative language means. Repeat with the other sentences. Invite students to share their illustrations with the rest of the class.

**INFORMAL ASSESSMENT**

Have students read the last sentence on page 581 and tell what they think "as light as air" means.

# Sequence of Events

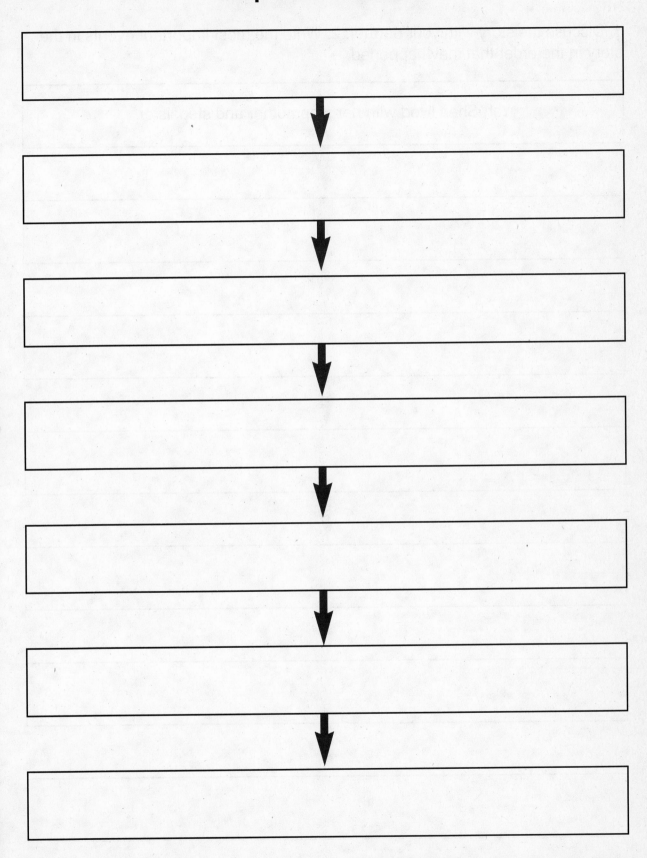

# Yeh-Shen, What Happened Then?

**1.** Discuss the story with your partner. **2.** Write the most important events in the story in the order that they happened.

Yeh-Shen lived with her stepmother and stepsister.

# What Will Happen to Yeh-Shen Next?

**1.** Color the picture that shows what you think will happen to Yeh-Shen and the King. **2.** Write a story telling what happens next on the lines below.

**Yeh-Shen and the King
Move to the Country.**

**Yeh-Shen and the King
Live Happily in the Palace.**

_____

_____

_____

_____

# Picture the Meaning

**1.** Draw a picture that explains each sentence. **2.** In your own words, write what you think each sentence means.

**1.** Yeh-Shen had dark pools for eyes.

_____

_____

**2.** Yeh-Shen had a heavy heart.

_____

_____

**3.** There was a shower of flying stones.

_____

_____

## BUILD BACKGROUND FOR LANGUAGE SUPPORT

# I. FOCUS ON READING

## Focus on Skills

### Develop Visual Literacy

**OBJECTIVE:** Important and unimportant information

Tell students that they are about to read an article on coral reefs. Then list the following information: *There are many coral reefs in the Caribbean. I have several shells in my shell collection. Many coral reefs are dying. My fish likes to swim in warm water.* Then ask students: *What information is important for understanding how to save the reefs?* Guide students to see that while all the information may be true, only some of the information is important for the stated purpose. Then turn students' attention to the Visual Literacy picture. As you look at the picture together, help students identify and name things they see. Guide them to distinguish between important and unimportant information in the sketch, by giving prompts such as: *Touch the pink plants in the picture of the coral reef. Do you think they're important to the picture? Point to something else you think is important. Fish are important in a picture of a coral reef. Show with your finger the direction some fish are swimming. Do you think the direction they are swimming is important to the picture?*

**TPR**

# II. READ THE LITERATURE

### Vocabulary

**VOCABULARY**
coral
reefs
percent
damage
loosened
ton

Write the vocabulary words on flashcards and distribute them to the students. Then display a picture of a coral reef and say the following sentences, pointing to parts of the picture as appropriate. Tell students to hold up the flashcard with the vocabulary word they hear in each sentence. *This is coral. It is the shell of tiny animals. Coral reefs are many corals put together. Put the pieces of coral together to make a reef. Percent means a part or portion. 50 percent is half. Take away 50 percent of the coral in our reef. Coral reefs are so tough that storms will not damage them. Show us what you think might damage a reef.* (Tie a knot in a piece of rope.) *Who will start to untie this? Ryan has loosened the knot for me. A ton is 2,000 pounds. Which weighs closer to a ton: a piece of coral or a car?* Then have students form small groups and read the sentences on Teacher Chart 145. Have each group find a picture, do a role-play, or create an illustration to show the meaning of each vocabulary word. Then have each group take turns demonstrating the meaning of each vocabulary word. Invite students to vote on which group's presentation is the most helpful.

### Evaluate Prior Knowledge

**CONCEPT**
coral reefs

Bring in pictures of coral reefs. Ask for volunteers to explain what they may already know about coral reefs. You may want to provide a world map so students can point to areas in the world where coral reefs can be found. Have students brainstorm a list of words which describe what they see in the pictures of the reefs. Then ask small groups of students to come up with one question they have about coral reefs. Have each group present their question to the rest of the class.

## Develop Oral Language

nonverbal prompt for active participation

one- or two-word response prompt

prompt for short answers to higher-level thinking skills

prompt for detailed answers to higher-level thinking skills

- Preproduction: Model and say: *Point to the picture of the coral reef. Does the coral reef grow underground? Does it grow underwater?*
- Early production: *Is coral a plant or an animal? Have you ever seen a coral reef up close? Can you name a place where you could find a coral reef?*
- Speech emergence: *Point to different types of coral in the reef? Can you name different shapes that appear in the reef? Can you name different colors in the reef?*
- Intermediate fluency: *Many coral reefs are endangered. Do you know why coral reefs may be dying? How does it make you feel to hear that the reefs are in danger? Do you think more people should know about this? Why?*

## Guided Instruction

### Preview and Predict

Tell students that the story they are going to read is about an endangered species. Read the title and have students preview the article. Use the photographs to reinforce the concept of endangered species and to encourage students to make predictions about what they will read. Ask questions such as: *What do we call this type of picture? Do you think this story is fact or fiction? Why? What do you see in a lot of the pictures? Which endangered species do you think this story is about? What other creatures might have problems because this species is endangered?* Discuss with students what they would like to learn from the article. For example: *What are coral reefs? Why are they endangered? What can we do to help them?* Record their questions on chart paper, and review them after reading the article to see whether they were answered.

**GRAPHIC ORGANIZER**
Blackline Master 97

### Objectives

- To distinguish between important and unimportant information
- To encourage critical thinking

### Materials

One copy of Blackline Master 97 per small group; pencils

Organize students in small groups and go over the chart headings together. After reading the title and first paragraph, ask students what the main idea of the article seems to be. Tell them that they will be looking for information that supports this main idea. Continue reading, stopping at the end of each section to let students record the most important facts from that section in the left column on their charts. Then have review what they have read and write unimportant information in the right column. Students needing extra language support can be grouped with more fluent English speakers who can take the role of recorder.

Have students go back to the list of questions they created about coral reefs. Using the chart of important and unimportant information, have students highlight or point to information which answers questions they may have had.

# III. BUILD SKILLS
## Comprehension

**REVIEW FACT AND OPINION**
Blackline Master 98

### Objectives
- To make, confirm, or revise predictions based on text
- To reinforce understanding of important information
- To encourage higher-level thinking skills

### Materials
One copy of Blackline Master 98 per student; pencils; crayons

Help students read the sentence in the first section. Ask them what they think will happen next. As they respond, write students' predictions on the board. Invite them to copy the sentences or phrases that tell what they think will happen next. They can then illustrate their predictions. Repeat with the other section on the page.

**INFORMAL ASSESSMENT**

Have students look at the photograph on page 605. Ask them what they think will happen to the fish in the picture if the coral reefs die.

## Vocabulary Strategy

**REVIEW FIGURATIVE LANGUAGE**
Blackline Master 99

### Objectives
- To identify and understand figurative language
- To encourage creative thinking
- To support hands-on learning

### Materials
One copy of Blackline Master 99 per student pair; scissors; pencils

Have students read the sentences in the left column. Discuss the meaning of each sentence, encouraging students to interpret the figurative language in their own words. Then read the sentences in the right column. Students can cut out the puzzle pieces, and work with their partners to match each figure of speech with its literal meaning. Challenge students to create a figure of speech and its literal meaning for the two puzzle pieces without text. Call on teams to share their figurative language with the group.

**INFORMAL ASSESSMENT**

Have students turn to page 604 and read the last paragraph. Have them find the sentence: *The reefs around Jamaica have been smothered by seaweed for years.* Encourage students to draw a picture illustrating this sentence. Then have students share their drawings with the class and discuss what words in the text influenced the way they drew their pictures.

# Vocabulary Strategy

**REVIEW CONTEXT CLUES**
Blackline Master 100

### Objectives

- To use context clues to define unfamiliar words
- To reinforce vocabulary

### Materials

One copy of Blackline Master 100 per student; pencils

Go over the column headings with students. Have them identify the first picture. Then ask them to look at the word and the missing letters in the next two columns, and write the missing letters on the correct lines. Repeat for the rest of the vocabulary words. Encourage students to use what they know about letter sounds as they complete the words. When they finish, have students work with partners to use each vocabulary word in a sentence.

**INFORMAL ASSESSMENT**

Direct students to page 605 and have them read the last paragraph. Write the word *delicate* on the chalkboard. Have students find the word in the paragraph and tell what it means. Encourage them to use context clues in the paragraph to find the meaning.

# Important and Unimportant Information

| IMPORTANT INFORMATION | UNIMPORTANT INFORMATION |
|---|---|
| | |

Name_____ Date_____

# Two Futures

**1.** Read the sentences below. **2.** Write what might happen next. **3.** Draw a picture to show what you think might happen.

**1.** A man clears an island forest so he can see a coral reef.

_____

_____

_____

**2.** A woman fisher sees a reef and decides not to fish there.

_____

_____

_____

Name_____ Date_____

# Matching Reefs

1. Cut out the pieces of the reefs. 2. Match up pieces that have the same meaning. 3. Match the blank pieces and write your own sentences to describe them.

| **What Is Said** | **What Is Meant** |
|---|---|

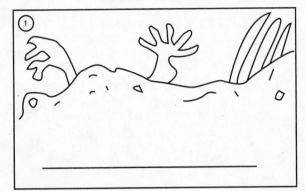

① 

_____

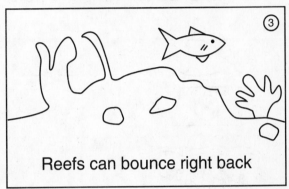

③ Reefs can bounce right back

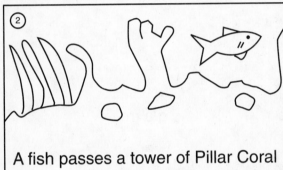

② A fish passes a tower of Pillar Coral

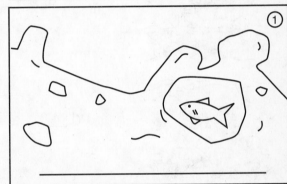

① 

_____

③ Reefs get better fast

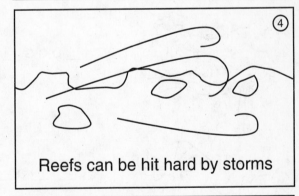

④ Reefs can be hit hard by storms

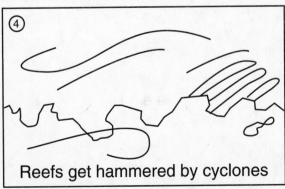

④ Reefs get hammered by cyclones

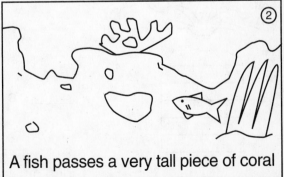

② A fish passes a very tall piece of coral

# Finish the Word

| Look at the picture. | Try to figure out the word. | Put the missing letters on the lines to complete the word. |
|---|---|---|

\_ o \_          n t

\_ e \_ \_ s          f r e

d \_ \_ a \_ e          g a m

\_ o o s \_ n i \_ \_          g n e l

c \_ \_ a \_          r l o

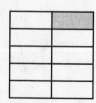
\_ \_ r c \_ n \_          e e p t

Written by Peter Golenbock Illustrated by Paul Bacon

## BUILD BACKGROUND FOR LANGUAGE SUPPORT

# I. FOCUS ON READING
## Focus on Skills

### Develop Visual Literacy

**OBJECTIVE:** Review cause and effect

**TPR**

Review with students cause and effect. Explain to students that a cause is what makes something happen and an effect is what happens. For an example, pantomime shivering and say: *What causes me to shiver?* Guide students to understand you are shivering because it is cold. Now direct students' attention to the painting. Have students point to the two women in the painting. Then have volunteers pair up and pose as the women in the painting. Ask the person on the right: *Why are you holding your hat like that?* Guide students to see that because it is windy, she is holding her hat on her head so it doesn't blow away. Then, ask questions such as: *Do you think the women in the picture are friends? What makes you think that? What might cause two people to walk in step? What effect does friendship have on how close you stand to someone? Point to something else in the picture that causes you to think the women are good friends.*

# II. READ THE LITERATURE

### Vocabulary

**VOCABULARY**
organizations
teammate
opponents
launched
extraordinary
circulated

Write each vocabulary word on a card. Hold up the card for a word as you say it and read the corresponding sentence from Teacher Chart 152. Use body language, repetition, and appropriate props to reinforce meanings. Then organize students into two teams to play Vocabulary Baseball. Draw a baseball diamond on the chalkboard. You will "pitch" vocabulary questions to team members. When a student answers correctly she or he runs their fingers around the diamond on the board as the team calls "Home Run!" Each correct answer scores one point. Ask questions or give directives such as: *Point to your teammates. Name the teammate next to you. Tell us the names of two of your opponents on the other team. Girl Scouts and Little League are organizations that some children belong to. Name other organizations you know of. Point in the direction a rocket goes when it is launched. An ordinary day is when nothing unusual happens. What could happen to make today extraordinary? Pass this piece of paper to everyone on your team and have each member write down their name. Which team circulated their list the fastest?*

### Evaluate Prior Knowledge

**CONCEPT**
friends to the end

To help students focus on the concept of friends to the end, have them work in groups of three. Give each group a problem situation involving friends, and have them dramatize the problem and the solution. Use each dramatization to reinforce the concepts of steadfastness, trustworthiness, reliability, that characterize good friendships. Examples of situations: *A bigger kid is teasing and pushing your friend. What do you do? What would you say if some kids asked you to go swimming, but said your best friend couldn't come? Show what you would do if your friend didn't want to play ball with you and some other children because she or he didn't know how.*

### Develop Oral Language

Have students draw a picture of a friend. Invite them to tell what makes this person a good friend. Discuss important qualities of friends.

nonverbal prompt for active participation

- Preproduction: *Show us* (point to self and class) *your friend* (point to picture). *Show us how your friend makes you feel* (point to your face).

one- or two-word response prompt

- Early production: *What is your friend's name? What do you like to do together? How do you feel when you're with your friend?*

prompt for short answers to higher-level thinking skills

- Speech emergence: *Who is your friend? Have you been friends long? How did you get to be friends? What do you like about your friend?*

prompt for detailed answers to higher-level thinking skills

- Intermediate fluency: *Tell us about your friend. Why are you friends? How long have you been friends? Tell us about a time a friend helped you get through a problem.*

# Guided Instruction

### Preview and Predict

Explain to students that this story is about Jackie Robinson, the first African American to become a famous baseball player. Have students preview the story. Use the illustrations to reinforce the concept of friends to the end and to make predictions about the story. Ask questions such as: *Who do you think the title Teammates is about? How can you tell this story is about a real person? What game are these men playing? What is different about the appearance of the players on the different teams? Why do you think these men are yelling? Why do you think this player has his arm around the other player?* Encourage students to talk about reasons to read the selection. For example: to find out more about Jackie Robinson; to learn more about baseball; to learn how friends can help each other through hard times.

**GRAPHIC ORGANIZER**
Blackline Master 101

### Objectives

- To identify cause and effect
- To encourage higher-level thinking skills
- To support cooperative group work

### Materials

One copy of Blackline Master 101 per student pair; pencils

Go over the chart headings with students. As you read the story, stop and have students identify causes and effects in what they read. For example, after reading page 619, discuss the segregation laws that existed before the 1940s. Have students identify how these laws affected the players of the Negro Leagues. Students can then work with their partners to write the cause and effect in the correct sections on their charts. Repeat the process with other parts of the story. Students needing additional language support can be paired with a more fluent speaker.

# III. BUILD SKILLS

## Comprehension

### REVIEW CAUSE AND EFFECT
Blackline Master 102

**Objectives**
- To identify cause and effect
- To encourage higher-level thinking skills

**Materials**

One copy of Blackline Master 102 per student; pencils

Have students read the first sentence in the *Cause* column. Then ask them to find the sentence or phrase in the right hand column that shows the effect of that cause. Students can then draw a line linking the cause and effect. Repeat with the other sentences on the page. When the page is complete, invite students to talk about how each cause led to each effect. Invite students to come up with cause-and-effect situations of their own.

**INFORMAL ASSESSMENT**

Have students read the second paragraph on p. 619. Ask students why fans came to see the Negro Leagues. (Because they had extraordinary players). Then read the last paragraph on the same page. Ask students: *What was the effect of the restaurant's refusal to serve black people.* (They had to buy meals that they could carry with them.)

## Comprehension

### REVIEW SUMMARIZING
Blackline Master 103

**Objectives**
- To review summarizing
- To analyze and make judgments and decisions
- To reinforce understanding of story characters

**Materials**

One copy of Blackline Master 103 per student; pencils; crayons

Have students read the first unfinished sentence. Ask them what important decision Jackie Robinson made in the story. Write their ideas on the chalkboard. Have students select the decision they think was most important and copy it onto their paper to complete the first sentence. Encourage students to make judgments about Jackie's decision. Help them write their ideas on the lines. Students can then illustrate the scene. Repeat the process for Pee Wee's decision.

**INFORMAL ASSESSMENT**

Direct students to the picture on page 625 of the crowd yelling. Ask them to identify what decision these men were making. Then call on students to judge whether or not they thought this was a good decision. Have them explain why they think as they do.

# Vocabulary Strategy

**REVIEW CONTEXT CLUES**
Blackline Master 104

## Objectives

• To use context clues to understand specialized vocabulary
• To support cooperative learning

## Materials

One copy of Blackline Master 104 per student; pencils

Have students work in small groups. Read the words at the top of the page and review their meanings together. Then have students work together to read the paragraph on the worksheet and fill in the missing words. Encourage students to point out context clues in the sentences around the missing word. Students can then write the appropriate vocabulary word on each line. Invite groups to choral read the completed story.

**INFORMAL ASSESSMENT**

Have students read the second paragraph on page 620. Write apathetic on the chalkboard, and have students find it in the text. Challenge them to find the meaning of the word by using context clues in the sentence and in the paragraph.

# Cause and Effect

| Cause | | Effect |
|-------|---|--------|

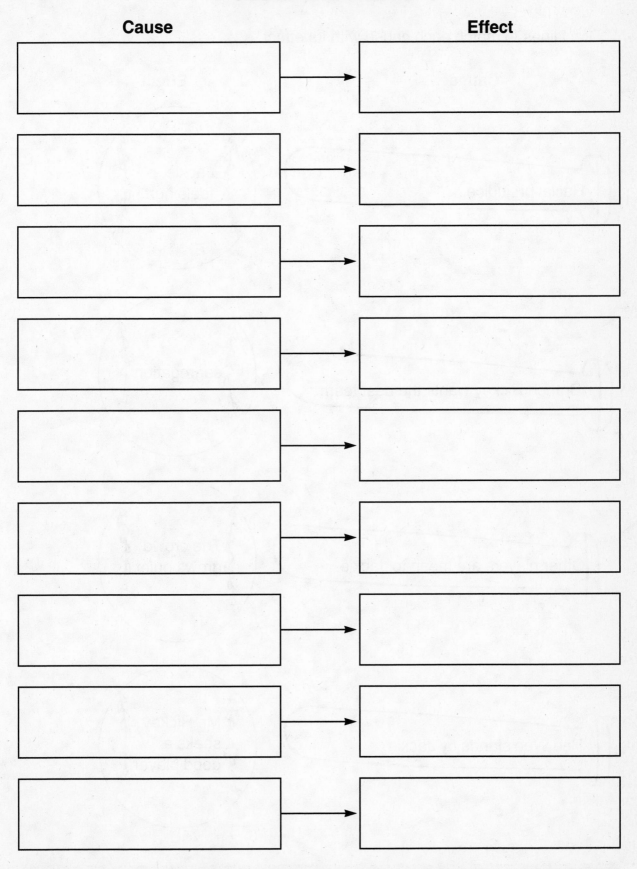

# Match Each Cause and Effect

**1.** Draw lines to match each cause with its effect.

**Cause**                                        **Effect**

Racial prejudice.

Jackie feels hurt.

Branch Rickey wants the best team.

segregation

Other players are mean to Jackie.

The crowd grows quiet.

Pee Wee stands by Jackie.

Mr. Rickey seeks a good player.

---

# Making Important Decisions

**1.** Finish each sentence below. **2.** Beneath the sentences draw a picture showing what is written about each person.

Jackie chose to _____.

It was hard because _____.

It was good because _____.

Pee Wee chose to _____.

It was hard because _____.

It was good because _____.

# Story of a Star

**1.** Read the story below. **2.** Copy the words listed below into the correct space to finish the story. **3.** Draw a picture of Fran and her new team underneath.

| opponents | teammates | search | league |
|---|---|---|---|

Once there was an extraordinary baseball player named Fran. The baseball _____ had many teams. Fran launched a _____ to see what team she wanted to play for. The players on the Sharks team were not nice. If she played for the Stars, her _____ would be nice to her. She would play for the Stars. The Sharks would be her _____ .That was okay. She knew the Stars would win.

# THE MALACHITE PALACE pp. 632A–663P

Written by Alma Flor Ada  Illustrated by Leonid Gore

## BUILD BACKGROUND FOR LANGUAGE SUPPORT

## I. FOCUS ON READING

### Focus on Skills

**OBJECTIVE:** Identify problems and solutions

**TPR**

### Develop Visual Literacy

Explain to students that many stories tell what happens when a character has a problem and looks for a solution. Arrange students in groups. Give each group a simple problem, such as: *you forgot your homework at home, you misplaced your house key, etc.* Have students work together to come up with a solution to each problem. Then have each group dramatize the problem and its solution for the rest of the class. Turn students' attention to the Visual Literacy painting. Help students name what they see in the picture. Write their responses on the board. Give prompts to help students focus on possible problems or solutions in the picture. For example: *Show us what might be wrong with the bird. What can the woman do to help? Can you think of another problem one of these characters might have? Show us how it could be solved.*

## II. READ THE LITERATURE

### Vocabulary

**VOCABULARY**
feeble
resembled
cultured
mingled
fragrance
scampered

Organize volunteers in front of the class. Read the sentences from Teaching Chart 158 and have the volunteers act out each sentence. Encourage the rest of the class to identify the vocabulary word in the sentence. Then have students suggest definitions and write them on the chalkboard. Reread the sentences, using their definitions to replace the vocabulary word in each sentence. Have students decide which definition fits the context clues. Then have students form small groups and interview each other. Have them make up questions using the vocabulary words. Model for the class, using these examples:

*Feeble:* Who is more likely to be <u>feeble</u>, an old man or a young man?

*Resemble:* Who do you <u>resemble</u> more, your mother or your father?

*Cultured:* Name someone famous who you think is <u>cultured</u>.

*Mingle:* Would you <u>mingle</u> at a party or by yourself?

*Fragrance:* What is your favorite <u>fragrance</u>?

*Scampered:* Name something that might have <u>scampered</u> in the woods.

### Evaluate Prior Knowledge

**CONCEPT**
royal families

Bring in pictures from fairy tales, books, newspapers, and so on, of different royal families. If possible, try to include royalty from cultures other than European. Help students identify the various members and discuss their roles. Encourage students to tell what they know of royal families from movies, television, books, and songs.

### Develop Oral Language

Have students work with a partner. Assign each pair an aspect of royal life to illustrate on paper. You might have them draw a picture of a royal family's home, what they do for fun, their work, clothing, food, and so on. Have them share their pictures with the rest of the group. Use prompts such as:

nonverbal prompt for active participation

- Preproduction: *Show us* (point to self and class) *your picture* (point to picture). *Point to where the princess sleeps.* (Point to princess and pantomime sleeping.) *Point to where the king sits.* (Point to king and pantomime sitting.)

one- or two-word response prompt

- Early production: *Show us your picture. What is the queen wearing on her head? Who else wears a crown? Do you think they wear crowns all the time? Are the royal family's clothes plain or fancy?*

prompt for short answers to higher-level thinking skills

- Speech emergence: *Tell us what you drew. What kinds of things do princes and princesses do for fun? How is that like what you do? How is it different? What do the queen and king like to do? Do your parents go to balls and banquets? What do your parents do for fun?*

prompt for detailed answers to higher-level thinking skills

- Intermediate fluency: *What kind of work does the king do? What kind of work doesn't he do? Who do you think cooks and cleans and fixes things around the palace? How is this different from what happens at your house? What work do you think the prince and princess have to do? How is this similar to or different from your life?*

## Guided Instruction

### Preview and Predict

Read the title of the story with students. Explain that malachite is a semi-precious green mineral. Then have students look at the illustrations in the story and make predictions about what they'll be reading. Ask questions such as: *What kind of people live in a palace? Who do you think this girl and these women are? How do you think the girl feels in this picture? Why do you think a princess might always be alone? What do you think the princess is doing with the bird? Why do you think she lets the bird go?* Invite students to discuss reasons for reading the story. For example, they might say they want to find out what it is like to be a princess; to learn why the princess let the bird go; or to find out what makes the princess look so happy at the end.

**GRAPHIC ORGANIZER**
Blackline Master 105

### Objectives

- To recognize problems and solutions
- To reinforce making judgments and decisions
- To encourage higher-level thinking skills

### Materials

One copy of Blackline Master 105 per student; pencils

Tell students that looking for details about a story's main problem will help them understand how the story unfolds. Remind students that a problem in a story is something the main character wants to change. The solution is how the character solves the problem. As you read the story, stop and ask students to identify what problem the princess is facing at that time, and how she attempts to solve it. Write suggestions on the chart on the chalkboard and have students copy them onto their *Problem and Solution* charts.

To reinforce the skill of making judgments and decisions, have students use the information on their charts to answer the following questions. Ask: *How did the princess finally solve her main problem of not having a friend? Do you think her solution was a good one? Explain your answer.*

# III. BUILD SKILLS

## Comprehension

### REVIEW PROBLEM AND SOLUTION
Blackline Master 106

**Objectives**
- To recognize problems and solutions
- To practice recalling story events
- To support hands-on learning

**Materials**

One copy of Blackline Master 106 per student; scissors; paste or glue

Review the worksheet with students and help them read the phrases in the left column. Have students cut out the solutions in the boxes at the bottom of the page. Then have students match each solution to the problem it solves. Invite volunteers to share their answers with the rest of the group. Discuss with students how most stories have at least one problem that needs to be solved, and that some solutions are better than others. Challenge students to think of other possible solutions to each problem.

**INFORMAL ASSESSMENT**

Have students reread page 643. Ask students to identify the problem with the bird and the solutions of the lady-in-waiting, the queen, and the governess.

## Comprehension

### REVIEW CAUSE AND EFFECT
Blackline Master 107

**Objectives**
- To identify causes and effects
- To reinforce understanding of story events

**Materials**

One copy of Blackline Master 107 per student pair; scissors

Read each phrase together with students. Help them identify the phrases on the left as story causes and the phrases on the right as story effects. Have students cut apart the boxes, turn them face down, and mix them up. Partners can then play a memory game by taking turns turning up two cards at a time to try to match a cause with its effect. If a match is made, the student keeps the cards. If no match is made, the student should turn the two cards face down again and let the other partner take a turn.

**INFORMAL ASSESSMENT**

Direct students to page 655. Have them identify what is happening in the picture. Ask them to tell what caused this to happen.

# Vocabulary Strategy

## Objectives

• To recognize synonyms and antonyms
• To understand word meanings

## Materials

One copy of Blackline Master 108 per student; red and blue crayons or colored pencils

Read the directions with students and review what alike and opposite mean. Have students read the first word in the left column. Explain that one of the words in the right column is either a synonym (alike) or antonym (opposite) of each word on the left. Have students draw a dotted line between words to match the synonyms and a solid line to match words that are antonyms. Be sure students understand they will only draw one line to and from each word. When the page is complete, ask students to name the words they found that were alike and those that were opposites.

**INFORMAL ASSESSMENT**

Have students read the paragraph on page 644. Write the word *joyful* on the board and have them find the word in the paragraph that means the opposite. (sad)

# Problem and Solution

**PROBLEM**

**ATTEMPTS**

**OUTCOMES**

**SOLUTION**

# Find the Solution

**1.** Cut out the solutions at the bottom of the page. **2.** Paste them next to the correct problem in the boxes below.

| Problem | Solution |
|---|---|
| **1.** Bird will not sing inside palace. | |
| **2.** Princess is sad without bird. | |
| **3.** Princess has no friends. | |

Princess runs out to play with children.

Princess makes cage into bird feeder.

Princess brings bird to window.

# Cause and Effect Pairs

1. Cut out each box below and turn it face down. 2. Turn 2 cards over at a time. 3. Find pairs of boxes that show cause and effect.

| | |
|---|---|
| Princess closes window. | Princess opens window. |
| Princess puts bird in cage. | Bird will not sing. |
| Bird hears children laugh. | Bird starts to sing again. |
| Princess hears tap on window. | Princess cannot hear children. |

## Alike and Opposite

**1.** Draw a dotted line to match words that are alike. **2.** Draw a solid line to match words that are opposites.

| | |
|---|---|
| red | hastily |
| open | indoors |
| outside | crimson |
| happy | closed |
| quickly | cultured |
| ignorant | joyful |

# THE TOOTHPASTE MILLIONAIRE pp. 664A–691P

Written by Jean Merrill  Illustrated by David Catrow

## BUILD BACKGROUND FOR LANGUAGE SUPPORT

# I. FOCUS ON READING

## Focus on Skills

### Develop Visual Literacy

**OBJECTIVE:** Make judgments and decisions

Look at the picture together, and have students identify what they see. Explain that this photograph is a scene from an old silent film called *Modern Times*. Ask students: *Point to the man who is trapped. Point to the man who must decide what to do to free the trapped man.* Invite students to take on the roles of machine, trapped man, and the man on the ladder to dramatize what they think will happen. Then return to the picture and encourage students to make judgments about the role of machinery in our lives. Ask questions such as: *What do you think is more important: people or machines? Who do you think should be in charge: people or machines? How do you think machines help us? Can they hurt us? What are some machines that you use everyday? Do you think machines are good or bad?*

**TPR**

# II. READ THE LITERATURE

### Vocabulary

**VOCABULARY**
commercials
gallon
ingredient
brilliant
successful
expensive

Write the vocabulary words on cards. Hold up each word as you use it in the following activities. Use repetition and body language to help students access meaning. Show students pictures or products that are advertised in popular commercials. Display a gallon milk carton, a quart milk carton, an empty ice cream carton, some self-stick notes, a book, and a toy car. Say: *I saw a commercial for soap on television last night. Which of these things have you seen commercials for?* Direct attention to the empty gallon milk carton and the quart carton. Say: *A gallon is more than a quart. Pick up the gallon container.* Point to the ice cream carton. Say: *Milk is an ingredient in ice cream. Can you name another ingredient used to make ice cream?* Hold up the self-stick notes. Say: *I think self-stick notes are great. The person who invented them had a brilliant idea. Can you think of any other brilliant inventions?* Point to the book. Say: *Doing homework will help you be successful in school. Show us something else you can do to be successful.* Hold up the toy car. Say: *A real car costs a lot of money; it is expensive. Point to something in this room that is expensive.* Then have students form small groups. Invite them to write their own commercials. Tell students to focus on a product, write a brief script, and include pictures or illustrations to accompany the text. Have students use all the vocabulary words in their script. Then have groups take turns presenting their commercials to the rest of the class.

### Evaluate Prior Knowledge

**CONCEPT**
kids making money

Bring in pictures of people doing different kinds of jobs. If possible, include pictures of kids working. Help students name the types of work depicted and any special clothing or equipment used to perform each job. As you hold up a picture, ask students to put their thumbs up if it is a job kids could do to make money. Encourage volunteers to describe or act out ways that they earn money.

### Develop Oral Language

Have students work in small groups to dramatize something kids can do to make money. Use prompts appropriate to students' linguistic levels. For example:

nonverbal prompt for active participation

one- or two-word response prompt

prompt for short answers to higher-level thinking skills

prompt for detailed answers to higher-level thinking skills

- Preproduction: *Show us* (point to self and class) *what you* (point to student) *could do to make money* (pantomime counting out money).

- Early production: *What job can kids do to make money? Have you done this job? Is it easy or hard? When do you do it?*

- Speech emergence: *What could you do to make money? What do you need to do this job? When do you do it? How do you do it? Who pays you for the job?*

- Intermediate fluency: *Tell us about a job kids could do to make money. How would you get what you need to start the job? How do you do the job? Do you need any help to do the work? How do you get paid for the job?*

## Guided Instruction

### Preview and Predict

Tell students that this selection is a play meant to be acted out. Read the title and explain that a millionaire is a person who has a million or more dollars. Have students take a picture walk to preview the selection. Use the pictures to reinforce the concept of kids making money and to encourage predictions. Ask questions such as: *Who do you think the millionaire is? How do you think he got his money? What do you think the boy is making in this picture? Why might he be making toothpaste? Why would the other kids help him? What do you think is being sold at the auction? What do you think this machine is doing? Why is this boy showing the toothpaste on television? Why do you think the play is called The Toothpaste Millionaire?* Help students make a list of what they hope to find out by reading the selection. For example: *How did the boy make a million dollars? How does toothpaste get made and sold?*

**GRAPHIC ORGANIZER**
Blackline Master 109

### Objectives

- To identify judgements and decisions
- To support ideas with details from the story

### Materials

One copy of Blackline Master 109 per student; pencils

Review the *Judgments and Decisions* chart with students. Remind them that making a decision involves judging different choices in a situation or evaluating pieces of information. As you read the play, stop and ask students to identify the judgments or decisions made by the characters. Then have students point out evidence from the text that supports their ideas. Record their suggestions on the chalkboard and have them copy them onto their papers.

For example, after reading p. 671 ask students: *What judgment does Rufus make about the price of toothpaste?* (He thinks its crazy to pay so much for toothpaste.) Then ask: *What decision does Rufus make?* (Rufus decides to make his own toothpaste.)

# III. BUILD SKILLS

## Comprehension

**REVIEW MAKE JUDGMENTS AND DECISIONS**
Blackline Master 110

### Objectives
- To identify judgments and decisions
- To support hands-on learning

### Materials
One copy of Blackline Master 110 per student; scissors

Review the worksheet with students and help them read each sentence. Tell students that when we make a judgment, or feel a certain way about something or someone, we often make decisions based on how we feel. Have students cut out the art on the page and match each judgment with the decisions that are made. When the page is complete, call on volunteers to share their answers with the group. Invite students to discuss judgments and decisions they have made.

**INFORMAL ASSESSMENT**

Direct students to page 684. Have them read the last ten lines where Mr. Perkell refuses to loan Rufus money. Ask students what judgment Mr. Perkell is making about kids. Then have them tell what decision he made, based on his judgment.

## Comprehension

**REVIEW PROBLEM AND SOLUTION**
Blackline Master 111

### Objectives
- To identify problems and solutions
- To encourage creative thinking

### Materials
One copy of Blackline Master 111 per student; colored pencils or crayons

Have students look at the picture in the first box on the worksheet and identify the problem. Then tell students to draw a solution to that problem in the second box. Then invite students to think of a problem they know how to solve. Have them draw a picture of this problem in the third box. They can exchange papers with a partner and challenge their partner to draw a solution to their problem in the fourth box. When the drawings are done, have partners compare solutions.

**INFORMAL ASSESSMENT**

Have students turn to page 685 and read the first column of text. Ask them to tell what Rufus' problem was, and how he solved it. (Rufus' problem is that the bank won't lend him money. He solves it by asking Hector to get the loan from the bank.)

# Vocabulary Strategy

## Objectives

• To identify synonyms and antonyms
• To build vocabulary

## Materials

One copy of Blackline Master 112 per student; scissors; paste or glue

Remind students that synonyms are words that have the same meaning and antonyms are words that have opposite meanings. Have students read the words on the toothbrushes. Tell them to cut out the words at the top of the page, and paste each one below its synonym or antonym. They can then color each pair of synonyms red and each pair of antonyms green. Invite students to read their word pairs to a partner.

**INFORMAL ASSESSMENT**

Have students read the stage directions at the top of page 670. Write the word small on the chalkboard and have students find it in the text. Ask them to find the word that has the opposite meaning of small. Then have students reread page 671. Point out the word started. Ask students to work together to think of a synonym and an antonym for the word *started*.

# Make Judgments and Decisions

| Judgment or Decision | Evidence from Story |
|---|---|
|  |  |

# How We Feel, What We Do

**1.** Read the sentences. **2.** Cut out the art. **3.** Put the pieces together to match judgments with decisions.

| Judgement | Decision |
|---|---|

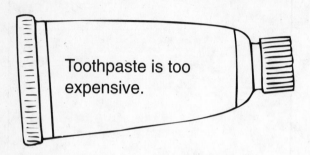

Toothpaste is too expensive.

Rufus gives Hector a job.

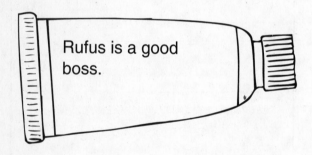

Rufus is a good boss.

Workers take stock instead of money from Rufus.

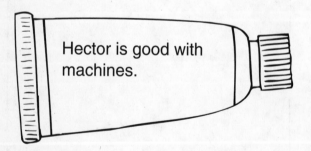

Hector is good with machines.

Rufus makes his own toothpaste.

# Amazing Toothpaste Solution

**Problem**

**Solution**

Draw a solution to this problem in the space below.

**Problem**

Draw a problem below that you know how to solve.

**Solution**

Give your drawing to your partner and ask him or her to draw a solution here.

# Squeeze a Word Match

**1.** Cut out the words. **2.** Paste each word on the handle of a toothbrush. **3.** Color the toothbrush red if the words have similar meanings. **4.** Color the toothbrush green if the words have opposite meanings.

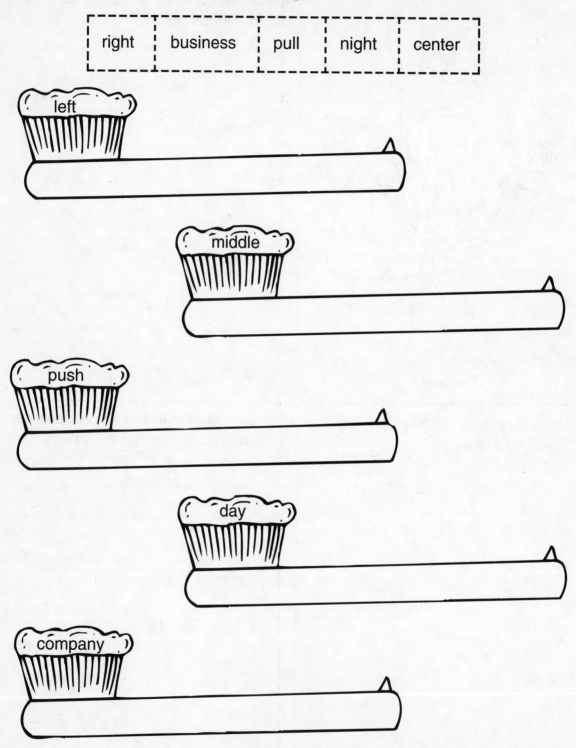

| right | business | pull | night | center |

left

middle

push

day

company

# WHALES pp. 692A–713P

Written by Seymour Simon

## BUILD BACKGROUND FOR LANGUAGE SUPPORT

## I. FOCUS ON READING

### Focus on Skills

#### Develop Visual Literacy

**OBJECTIVE:** Review compare and contrast

Look at the painting *Fighting Cows*. Have students name the animals they see. Encourage them to compare and contrast elements in the picture by giving prompts such as: *Put your fingers on the two main animals in the picture. What are they doing? Touch something on both cows that is similar. How are the cows alike? Now point to something that is different between the two cows. How are the cows different from the other animals in the picture? How are they the same?* Have students tell if they have ever seen cows in real life. Ask: *How are the cows in the painting different from the cows you saw? How are they the same?*

**TPR**

Then have students draw their own illustration of "Fighting Cows." Ask volunteers to show their drawings to the rest of the class. Have the class compare and contrast students' paintings to the one by Franz Marc.

## II. READ THE LITERATURE

### Vocabulary

**VOCABULARY**
marine
identify
related
pods
mammals
preserve

Write the vocabulary words on the chalkboard. Frame each word as you use it in the following activities. Show students pictures of different kinds of whales. Include pictures of pods as well as pictures of single whales. Say: *Stand and tell us the name of these animals that live in the ocean. What other marine animals do you know of? How many whales can you identify in this picture? Point to the baby whale and its mother. These two whales are related. They are family. Who are you related to? Whales often hunt in family groups called pods. Show me with your fingers how many pods you see in these pictures. Whales are mammals because they are warm blooded and nurse their babies. Pretend you are another type of mammal and we'll try to guess what you are. People are trying to preserve whales by making laws against hunting them. Can you name any other animals we must preserve?* Then have students gather in small groups and assign each group a vocabulary word. Have each group create an illustration of the vocabulary word and use that word in a context sentence. Have groups take turns presenting sentences and illustrations to the rest of the class.

### Evaluate Prior Knowledge

**CONCEPT**
endangered animals

Bring in pictures of endangered species of whales. Help students name the types of whales they see. Explain that these whales are endangered. Encourage students to recall what they learned about endangered species in a previous unit. Ask students to think of other animals which are endangered. You may want students to work in groups to do some preliminary research on endangered animals in an encyclopedia or on the Internet. Invite students to find a picture in a magazine or create their own picture of an endangered animal.

## Develop Oral Language

Have students work with a partner. Each pair of students will present a picture of an endangered animal to the rest of the class. In addition, students will present facts about why the animal is endangered, where it lives, etc.

nonverbal prompt for active participation

- Preproduction: *Show us the picture of your animal. Is this animal endangered? Can you write the name of the animal on the chalkboard? Is the animal big or small? Show us how big (use your hands) the animal is.*

one- or two-word response prompt

- Early production: *Can you tell us where the animal lives? Have you ever seen this animal in nature? Have you seen it in a zoo?*

prompt for short answers to higher-level thinking skills

- Speech emergence: *Can you tell us why this animal is endangered? Do people hunt this animal? Do other animals hunt this animal?*

prompt for detailed answers to higher-level thinking skills

- Intermediate fluency: *What can be done to protect this animal from extinction? Do you know if there is an organization who protects these animals? Where can we find out more information on this animal?*

# Guided Instruction

## Preview and Predict

Read the title and the author's name with students. Ask them what they think the story will be about. Then have students preview the story by looking at the photographs. Encourage students to make predictions. Ask questions such as: *What do we call these kind of pictures? What does this photograph show? Do you think this story is fact or fiction? Why? Are all the whales alike? How are they different? What do you think these whales are doing? What do you think might happen to this whale if the water was polluted? What do you think this whale eats? Why do you think this?* Encourage students to talk about reasons for reading the selection. For example, they might say they want to learn more about whales and why some are endangered.

## Objectives

**GRAPHIC ORGANIZER**
Blackline Master 113

- To compare and contrast information
- To identify main idea and supporting details
- To encourage higher-level thinking skills

## Materials

One copy of Blackline Master 113 per small group; pencils

Explain to students that as they read this selection, they will compare and contrast information to find similarities and differences among different types of whales. Read the chart headings together. As you read the story, stop and ask students specific questions to help them compare or contrast whales. For example: *How are all whales alike? What is the difference between toothed whales and baleen whales? How are male and female sperm whales alike? How are they different?* Students can work in small groups to record their ideas on the charts. Students who need extra language support can be grouped with more fluent speakers.

# III. BUILD SKILLS

## Comprehension

### REVIEW COMPARE AND CONTRAST
Blackline Master 114

**Objectives**
- To make comparisons and contrasts
- To recall story details

**Materials**

One copy of Blackline Master 114 per student; pencils

Help students read the chart headings. As a group, read the first description in the column *What I Learned About the Whale*. Students can look back through the text to find the name of the whale which matches the description. Have students write the name of that whale either in the column labeled Toothed or the one labeled Baleen. Repeat with the other descriptions on the page. Encourage students to use their completed charts to talk about how individual whales are similar or different.

### INFORMAL ASSESSMENT

Direct students to page 696 and have them read the second paragraph. Then have them read the second sentence at the top of page 700. Now ask students to find two differences between toothed and baleen whales. (Toothed whales have teeth while baleen whales have baleen plates; Toothed whales feed on fish and squid while baleen whales feed on tiny sea creatures; Toothed whales have one blowhole while baleen whales have a two-part nostril or blowhole.)

## Comprehension

### REVIEW JUDGMENTS AND DECISIONS
Blackline Master 115

**Objectives**
- To make judgments and decisions
- To encourage creative thinking
- To make predictions

**Materials**

One copy of Blackline Master 115 per group of three students; scissors; craft sticks or pencils; tape or paste

Review with students the pictures on the worksheet. Help them identify the pictures as a whaler, a marine biologist, and a whale. In groups of three, have students cut each picture and tape or paste them to sticks or pencils. Then have students act out short plays about the future of whales. Encourage students to consider the judgments each character has about whales, and the kinds of decisions they might make based on these judgments. Invite each group to perform their play for the rest of the class.

### INFORMAL ASSESSMENT

Have students read the first paragraph on page 708. Challenge students to identify the judgments behind the IWC's decision to ban commercial whaling. Then ask: *The governments of a few countries still allow whale hunting. What decisions do you think these governments have made about whales to influence their decision?*

# Vocabulary Strategy

**REVIEW CONTEXT CLUES**
Blackline Master 116

## Objectives

- To use context clues to figure out meaning of words
- To reinforce understanding of specialized vocabulary
- To support recall of story details

## Materials

One copy of Blackline Master 116 per student; pencils

Go over the directions together. Have students read the first sentence. Explain that the letters in the right column are the missing letters to the incomplete word from the sentence. To help students complete the word, encourage them to use context clues from the sentence as they recall details about what they read.

**INFORMAL ASSESSMENT**

Write the word *accustomed* on the chalkboard. Have students read the last paragraph on page 706 and find *accustomed* in the text. Ask them to use context clues to figure out the meaning of the word.

# Compare and Contrast

<table>
<tr><td colspan="2"></td></tr>
<tr><td>**Similarities**</td><td>**Differences**</td></tr>
</table>

<table>
<tr><td colspan="2"></td></tr>
<tr><td>**Similarities**</td><td>**Differences**</td></tr>
</table>

<table>
<tr><td colspan="2"></td></tr>
<tr><td>**Similarities**</td><td>**Differences**</td></tr>
</table>

Name_____ Date_____

# Comparing Whales

| Name | | What I Learned About the Whale |
|---|---|---|
| **Toothed** | **Baleen** | |
| | | The male grows to sixty feet long. The female to only 40 feet. It is a slow swimmer, champion diver and likes to eat squid. It can stay underwater for over an hour. |
| | | A leopard-spotted whale approximately 15 feet long. The male has a 10 foot long tooth that grows through the upper lip and sticks out. They live along the edge of the sea ice in the Arctic. |
| | | It is the largest member of the dolphin family. It can grow over 30 feet and weigh 9 tons. They are found all over the world. They eat fish, squid, seal and other mammals. |
| | | They can grow to 50 feet and weigh as much as 70 tons. They have large flippers and a long lower lip. They each have their own pattern of small bumps on their heads. |
| | | It swims on its side on the bottom of the ocean to catch food. They live only in the North Pacific. The females give birth in the warm lagoons of Baja California. |
| | | It has a long body, a pointed head and thin flukes. The Fin whale is a fast swimmer. They work in pairs to catch food. They can grow to become nearly 90 feet long. |
| | | The blue whale is bigger than the largest dinosaur that ever lived. In one day a blue whale eats more than 4 tons of krill. Only a few can be found in the Antarctic. |
| | | The males sing songs that might attract female humpbacks. The songs last up to 30 minutes. |

# What Will We Do?

1. Cut out each picture. 2. Paste each picture to a stick to make a puppet.
3. Make a play to tell about the future of whales.

# Finish the Whale Words

1. Read the sentences below. 2. Each sentence has an incomplete word. 3. Use the letters on the right side of the page to fill in the blanks.

1. A toothed whale has one b __ __ w __ o __ __ __.    o l e l h

2. Orcas can be found in __ __ r i __ __ parks.    n e a m

3. A group of whales is called a __ __ d.    o p

4. Whales are sea __ a m __ a __ __.    m s m l

5. Right whales __ k __ __ the water.    m s i

6. Right whales have big f __ i __ p __ __ __.    p l r e s

# SAVING THE EVERGLADES pp. 714A–723P

Time For Kids

## BUILD BACKGROUND FOR LANGUAGE SUPPORT

## I. FOCUS ON READING

### Focus on Skills

**Develop Visual Literacy**

**OBJECTIVE:** Review cause and effect

Review with students the concept of cause and effect. Show students a picture of a forest and then one of a forest destroyed by fire. Ask students to compare the two forests. Point to the second picture and ask: *What do you think caused this to happen? What effect does fire have on the forest?* Then turn students' attention to the picture *Caribbean Jungle.* Have students name what they see in the picture. To help review cause and effect, give students directives such as: *Are the colors in this painting bright or dark? What effect do bright colors have on you? Point to two different sized trees? Which one is bigger? What caused this tree to grow bigger than the other one? Show us how you feel about the scene in the picture? Do you like it? What effect do you think the artist wants the painting to have on the viewer? What may have caused her to paint this picture?*

**TPR**

## II. READ THE LITERATURE

### Vocabulary

**VOCABULARY**
lurk
soggy
wildlife
instance
importance
compares

Write the vocabulary words on the chalkboard. Frame each word as you use it in the following activity. Use body language and repetition to help students assess meaning. Ask questions or give prompts such as:

*This is how a bank robber would lurk around a building so no one would see him.* Model lurking behavior. Then say: *Now you pretend to lurk. Why else might a person lurk?*

Dramatize the process of fixing a bowl of cereal. Say: *If I put too much milk in here, my cereal will be soggy. How do you look when you eat soggy cereal? What else have you eaten that was soggy?*

Show a picture of a snake or of a jungle scene. Say: *There are snakes in the jungle. What other kinds of wildlife might you see in a jungle? You can see wildlife in other places, too.*

*For instance, people see tigers in circuses and zoos.* Ask: *What is another instance where you might see animals?*

Show a picture of a baseball team. Point to the umpire, the catcher, the batter, the pitcher, the coach. Ask: *Which position is of the most importance to winning the game: the catcher, batter, pitcher, or umpire?* Point to the batter and ask: *Which is of more importance to the batter: to hit the ball far or to catch the ball?* Repeat with other positions.

Point to a boy and a girl student. Say: *If (name of girl) compares herself to (name of boy), what does she find? Is she taller? If she compares herself to another student, what does she find? How are they alike? How are they different?*

Then have students work in small groups. Give each group a vocabulary word, and have them make up a sentence using that word. Groups can share their sentences with the class.

## Evaluate Prior Knowledge

**CONCEPT**
conservation

Review with students what they may already know about endangered creatures and environments. Make a list of things that endanger Earth as well as some living creatures. Use pictures or props to help students see some of the causes of these dangers. Then brainstorm various conservation measures that people can take to help preserve the environment. Ask students what they know about efforts to preserve and protect Earth and its living creatures. For example: reuse, reduce, recycle. Have students work in small groups. Each group can choose one of the problems from the list above, and dramatize the problem and a conservation measure to solve it. Encourage students to come up with conservation ideas of things they can do themselves.

## Develop Oral Language

Ask questions such as:

nonverbal prompt for active participation

- Preproduction: Model and say: *Show us what the problem is. Show us what we can do to solve this problem.*

one- or two-word response prompt

- Early production: *Show us the problem. Where should we put our garbage so Earth will be cleaner? What can we do with cans and bottles?*

prompt for short answers to higher-level thinking skills

- Speech emergence: *What is the problem? What caused the water pollution? What things can help clean up the water? What can we do when we visit a river or lake or the ocean?*

prompt for detailed answers to higher-level thinking skills

- Intermediate fluency: *Tell us about the problem. What caused the air to be polluted? How does this effect people and other living things? What can people do instead of using their cars so much? What can we do if a factory is polluting the air?*

# Guided Instruction

## Preview and Predict

Have students read the title of the article. Explain that the Everglades is a swampy area in Florida. Preview the selection by reviewing the pictures in the selection with the students. Use the photographs to reinforce the concept of conservation and to encourage students to make predictions. Ask questions such as: *Where do you think the Everglades are? What do you think the Everglades look like? What animals do you think live there? Why might the Everglades need to be saved? What do you think caused some of the problems in the Everglades? Why do you think this? Do you think this story is fact or fiction? Why?* Help students make a list of what they hope to learn by reading the article. Refer back to the list after reading the selection to see whether their questions were answered or require further research.

**GRAPHIC ORGANIZER**
Blackline Master 117

## Objectives

- To practice identifying cause and effect
- To reinforce understanding of judgments and decisions
- To encourage higher-level thinking skills

## Materials

One copy of Blackline Master 117 per student; pencils

Go over the chart headings with students. Remind them that a cause is why something happens, and an effect is what happens. As you read, ask students to identify some of the problems in the Everglades. Write their ideas on the board and have them copy them in the *Effect* column on their papers. Then ask students to identify a cause for each problem. Help them record these in the *Cause* column on their charts. Now ask students to recall some of the solutions that are being tried. Students can record these under the *Cause* column. The effects of each solution can be written in the *Effect* column.

To reinforce the skill of making judgments and decisions, ask students whether they think it was a good idea for farmers to use fertilizers to help their crops grow. Have them explain their answers.

# III. BUILD SKILLS

## Comprehension

**REVIEW COMPARE AND CONTRAST**
Blackline Master 118

**Objectives**
• To review compare and contrast
• To practice recalling story details
• To support following directions

**Materials**
One copy of Blackline Master 118 per student; crayons or colored pencils; pencils

Read the directions and the scene headings together as a class. Have students recall descriptions of the Everglades at different points in time. Then have students illustrate each scene according to the descriptions in the selection, and write a sentence about it. Invite students to share their drawings with the rest of the group. Encourage students to compare and contrast the Everglades over the years as they discuss the changes that have occurred.

**INFORMAL ASSESSMENT**

Direct students to page 719. Have students read the text about alligators and crocodiles. Then have them compare and contrast the two animals.

## Vocabulary Strategy

**REVIEW SYNONYMS AND ANTONYMS**
Blackline Master 119

**Objectives**
• To practice identifying synonyms and antonyms
• To reinforce story vocabulary
• To support hands-on learning

**Materials**
One copy of Blackline Master 119 per student; orange and purple pencils or crayons

Have students read the words on the worksheet. Encourage students to see how some of the words mean the same thing and some words have opposite meaning. Have students read a word in the scene, and then find another word that has either the same or the opposite meaning. Have students draw orange lines between words that are alike and purple lines between words that are opposites. Finally, challenge students to make up sentences using the words on the page.

**INFORMAL ASSESSMENT**

Direct students' attention to page 717. Read the third sentence in the third paragraph. Have students think of a synonym and an antonym for the word *bad*. Talk about how these words affect the meaning of the sentence.

# Vocabulary Strategy

**REVIEW CONTEXT CLUES**
Blackline Master 120

## Objectives

- To practice using context clues
- To reinforce story vocabulary
- To support cooperative learning

## Materials

One copy of Blackline Master 120 per student; pencils; crayons or colored pencils

Have students read the words at the top of the page. Let them work in groups to read the story and then use context clues to fill in the missing words. Then have students draw a picture of the swamp. When the pictures are complete, invite groups to choral read the story and show their illustrations.

**INFORMAL ASSESSMENT**

Direct students' attention to the third sentence on page 717. Write the sentence on the chalkboard: *A few trees dot the landscape under the Florida sun.* Have students use context clues to figure out the meaning of the word *landscape.*

# Cause and Effect

| CAUSE | EFFECT |
|-------|--------|
|       |        |
|       |        |
|       |        |
|       |        |

# Change and Stay the Same

**1.** Color a picture for each scene. **2.** Write a sentence about each scene.

**The Everglades long ago.**

**The Everglades in the 1920's.**

**The Everglades today.**

# River of Grass, Swamp of Cattails

**1.** Read the words in the picture below. **2.** Underline words that are alike. **3.** Draw a dotted line between words that are opposite.

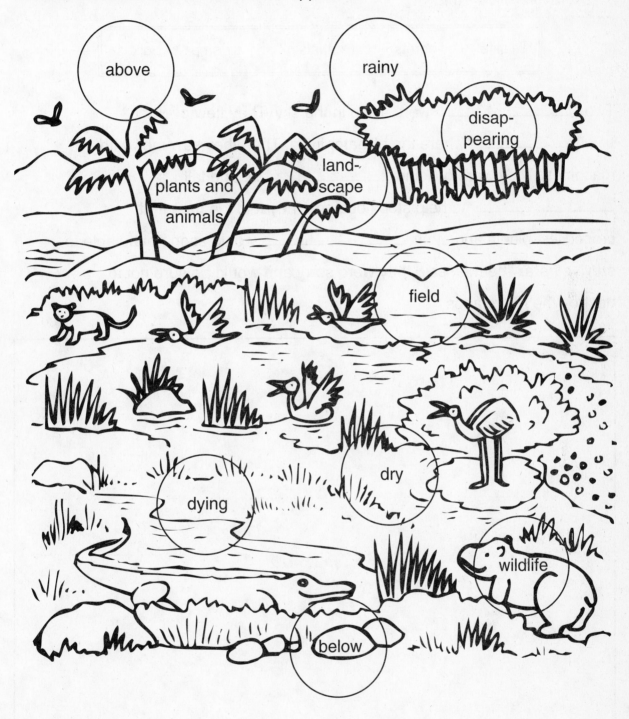

Name_____ Date_____

# A Swampy Story

**1.** Read the story below. **2.** Fill in words in the blanks to finish the story. **3.** Draw a picture of the swamp.

| wildlife | egrets | canals | swamp | dikes |

Two _____ were flying in the sky. They flew over the

_____ where the alligator lived. Then they saw men with

machines. They were building _____ and tall

_____ to help stop flooding. They told the men that

crocodiles, plants and other _____ would soon not be able to

survive here. The men said they were sorry and would be sure not to

destroy the Everglades.